Creative Writing

By the same author:

Poetry: This I Say
The Fifth Horseman of the Apocalypse
Adrift on the Star Brow of Taliesin
Double Image (poem posters)
Bone Harvest Done
Wild Children
Grotesque Tournament and Other Poems

Prose: Concorde File (teenage novel)
The Way to Write (with John Moat)

Anthologies: Listen to This (schools)
Stop and Listen (schools)
Horizons (schools)
Frontier of Going

Creative Writing

JOHN FAIRFAX

Elm Tree Books . London

ELM TREE BOOKS

Published by the Penguin Group
27 Wrights Lane, London W8 5TZ, England
Viking Penguin Inc, 40 West 23rd Street, New York, New York 10010, U.S.A.
Penguin Books Australia Ltd, Ringwood, Victoria, Australia
Penguin Books Canada Ltd, 2801 John Street, Markham, Ontario, Canada L3R 1B4
Penguin Books (N.Z.) Ltd, 182–190 Wairau Road, Auckland 10, New Zealand

Penguin Books Ltd, Registered Offices: Harmondsworth, Middlesex, England

First published in Great Britain 1989 by
Elm Tree Books Ltd
27 Wrights Lane, London W8 5TZ

British Library Cataloguing in Publication Data

ISBN 0-241-12576-6 HB
0-241-12577-4 PB

Printed and bound in Great Britain by
Butler and Tanner Ltd, Frome, Somerset

Contents

Acknowledgements

It would be difficult to list the people who have helped, in one way or another, with this book, especially all the would-be writers who attended courses, sessions, and workshops. To them I owe thanks. I also wish to thank those writer-tutors with whom I've worked.

My uncle presented me with Robert Louis Stevenson's Essays in the Art of Writing when I was sixteen. The quotes from the book I've underlined and chewed on since then.

The one person I must name is Sue Stewart for her unstinting help while putting this book together. The book is dedicated to Sue.

Every effort has been made to contact students for permission to use their writings. If any have been inadvertently missed I apologize and if they contact me I will gladly acknowledge them.

J.F.

Introduction

The artist must now step down, don his working clothes, and become the artisan. He now resolutely commits his airy conception, his delicate Ariel, to the touch of matter; he must decide, almost in a breath, the scale, the style, the spirit, and the particularity of execution of his whole design.

Robert Louis Stevenson

Creative Writing is a phrase, almost a buzz phrase, which is open to a number of interpretations. These range from instant self-expressive writing to poetry and prose which has been drafted and crafted to a polished and complete piece of work.

When I started to write I was hugely fortunate to know older writers who took me under their wings and gave me an invaluable apprenticeship. There was one occasion when one of my mentors plucked a blade of grass from a tuft on a Cornish clifftop and told me to write about that single piece of vegetation. I'd been expecting some marvellous all-comprehending theme that I could wallow in. Instead I had six inches of common light green grass. My mentor said, 'Write me this grass so that I would recognize it from other grass.'

To say that I was disappointed with this challenge would be an understatement. I had expected Olympian themes to roll a glorious phalanx of words and images into the arena. Instead a piece of mean grass!

As I walked away clutching the single blade I began to let ideas form. By the time I arrived at my cottage that blade had grown into something else. The roots held the soil and stopped it from eroding and blowing in the wind. It gave colour to the land. By binding the soil it allowed other plants to grow. The grass fed all manner of creatures, and man hunted and husbanded those creatures. Civilisation – in a blade of grass.

By the time I sat over my notebook that single blade had become such a vast theme that I wondered if I would ever finish writing about it. I don't recall that I ever did write about grass but it was a starting post; it set the ideas and words spinning. And since I showed my mentors the things I wrote I must have come up with something: they certainly would have encouraged, cajoled, shamed and bullied me into it.

If you want to learn a craft you sensibly go to a person who knows how to do it. Preferably someone with a track record and the ability, enthusiasm, patience, imagination and unselfishness to offer his/her knowledge, understanding and skill. If you want to learn to juggle you'd find a juggler, rather than a charcoal burner, to teach you. If you want to fly you'd go to a professional pilot at a flying school. If you want to learn mountaineering you'd be well advised to seek out a mountaineer. Young artists can go to art college. Musicians have their academies and colleges.

What of persons who want to write? One thing they can do is spend time at Arvon* where they will be able to work with practising writers as tutors. John Moat and I founded The Arvon Foundation in 1968 and there are now two Centres, one in Devon, the other in Yorkshire, where five day Courses in Creative Writing are held. The essential, and only, qualification students require is that they are seriously interested in writing. Both Centres cater for students through a wide range of age and ability. There are Creative Writing Courses specifically for schools, as well as Open Courses for anyone who wishes to attend. Because the people who attend Arvon are engaged solely with writing, the five days can be intensely creative.

* The Arvon Foundation: Totleigh Barton, Sheepwash, Beaworthy, Devon EX21 5NS
Lumb Bank, Hebden Bridge, Heptonstall, West Yorkshire HX7 6DF.

There are also creative writing groups around the country, many of which are run by practising writers. (Contact your regional arts association for details.)

This book has been put together in an attempt to help those who want to write and need a jump start. All the exercises, themes, games, and word play, have been used at one time or another over the years to help young (that is, beginning) writers delve among the words, to play with them and get the hang of stringing them into phrase, sentence, paragraph – or image, stanza, verse – to become familiar with, and even love the idea of what words can achieve for them on the page.

Teaching someone to write is a different ball game. That is not the point of this book. This book is for those who want to enjoy the rough and tumble of words, who want to get among them and see what happens.

For more than twenty years I've tutored creative writing courses – in schools, universities and arts workshops, with pupils, inservice teachers and private students – and have encouraged writers of various ages and abilities, all the while continuing with my own writing. It is important to me that I write. I think it would be shameful for me to get others to write if I were not doing so myself.

Helping someone to write creatively is a subtle exercise. The student's room for success – or error – is wider than if he or she were, for instance, learning to walk the tightrope. If they miss their footing on a rope, they fall off. But how do writers find their feet creatively? There's the grammar, syntax and meaning to control. There's the rhythm, pace and tone, the weight, colour and depth; there's the heart, spirit and energy. There's the word, the word, the word. And – the most subtle thing of all – there is the unique 'voice', the one totally personal way of saying/writing what he or she wants to write.

The teacher of creative writing needs to know his or her student well enough to let the poised pen find its own pace, its own territory, its own special direction. This is not to suggest that the work should not subscribe to the rules of

3

grammar. Or spelling. What it does mean is that those writing creatively should be unshackled by prescribed ideas, logic or reason. They should be invited to allow their ideas to flow and their imaginations to ride those ideas. The tutor must be free enough in him/herself to be able to see someone prospecting with language and let them go, while at the same time being aware of the map the student is charting.

One time while I was doing a stint as creative writing tutor at Reading Jail (the ghost of Oscar Wilde whispering in my ear) a remand prisoner asked if he could show me his plea of mitigation – as a piece of writing. He worked on it for a couple of weeks, casting and recasting paragraphs he felt unsatisfied with, then sentences, and finally the occasional word. One day his solicitor arrived, and the prisoner took his plea to him. Just before I left he returned and said that the solicitor had told him it was the best written plea he'd ever seen. The prisoner looked doubtful and said to me, 'I think I can get a couple of these lines better.' He went to a table and chewed his pen over the sentences he wanted to recast. My job finished before he went for trial, so I don't know how the court reacted to his plea.

Also at Reading Jail, a young Nigerian asked me to suggest something he might write, adding that he wasn't too good at English. I suggested he write the words that made him picture what he wanted to say, perhaps a few lines about something important to him, close to his home. A week later he showed me about fourteen lines of prose on lined, thin, prison paper which captured a picture of a magical pool near his village. Unhappily I was not permitted to copy or take out any of the writings but I remember the heartbreak in that man's tortured English as he relived and wrote of the boulder in the middle of the pool that turned the water golden, and of the fish grown huge because of the village taboo about taking them from the water.

Creative writing is not a therapy or placebo: there's much more to it than that. But the creative use of language can be a way for the individual to identify him/herself and gain

4

confidence from the expression of that self. As Professor J Z Young writes in his book, *Programs of The Brain*, 'the most important universal feature of all is the creativity or productivity of language. The fact that we can construct and understand an indefinitely large number of messages is the basis of the freedom of the individual to be different from others.'

What seems to be so often forgotten is that the one creative expression common to most people, of whatever age and ability, is their language. There is a fine art in using it, whether for a poem or letter, for telling a story or joke. Properly provided for and developed, language carries in it both art and craft.

It's tempting to plunge into what creative writing might achieve. Heaven knows what realms could be explored. However, the remit of this book is simply to give/offer some tempting morsels for people to let *their* language, voices, brains and imaginations pick at.

The last thing this little book sets out to do in any way whatsoever is to restrict, anchor, hamper or place any barrier between the individual, with pen poised, and his/her 'found' subject. The prime aim, maybe the sole aim, is to give some exercises as a battery boost to and for those who, when confronted by the white sheet of paper, freeze, go blank, or find their brains scramble and words skitter into the void.

Play with words – have fun with them. Words respond. They like tumbling about, they like the sounds they make, the tunes they dance to and the meanings they construct.

Many people are put off writing because they are or were told they must write in a particular fashion. Who says so? If we all wrote the same way there would be only one poem, one book, one play. One is one and all alone. And, as a matter of plain fact, the language would very soon dry up. Be obsolete.

Having fun with language does not in the least preclude writing seriously. There are probably more serious things to write about than there are frivolous, humorous, or down-

5

right nuts. Let me transmute the idea of having fun with language, and the exercises set out in the following pages, into the animal kingdom. A lioness with cubs. The cubs cuff one another, bite at each other's necks, trip up brother and sister and generally look as if they're having a ball. They probably are; but underlying their play is the serious business of learning. They are learning how to survive when it's their turn to hunt and kill.

I'm not promoting the idea that we use language or writing to kill, but it is a weapon – although I'd rather call it a tool. With language we make something, be it a note asking the coalman to leave us a sack of smokeless fuel, a letter to a friend telling them where to meet you in a town they don't know, or a complaint to the tax office about the miserable inadequacy of your overdue rebate. Whatever you write, it is of some importance to make your meaning clear.

When a poem or story is completed, something else is added to the alchemy of language. The poem or story becomes something more than the sum of its parts; somewhere along the way the intangible slides in.

Each of the wordspinners in this book can be adapted to suit most groups, from primary school pupils to adult writers. As I have stressed, age and ability should not be a consideration when using this book.

Here we're about words, and about being creative with them.

Co-operate

(A writer) goes on unafraid, laying down the law; and he is sure at heart that most of what he says is demonstrably false, and much of a mingled strain, and some hurtful, and very little good for service; but he is sure besides that when his words fall into the hands of any genuine reader, they will be weighed and winnowed, and only that which suits will be assimilated . . .

Robert Louis Stevenson

A while ago I read an essay on a philosophy which called itself *Nice Guys Win*. If my memory is trustworthy the thrust of the theory is that by co-operating rather than competing with others the co-operators will gain most. Since this book, Heaven forfend, isn't a philosophical treatise I don't in any manner feel obliged to go further into *Nice Guys Win*. However, the following creative writing exercise does in a way have a bearing on the idea.

This writing teaser works most fruitfully with groups of people, and it is easiest if there are even numbers.

Since naming names is the writer's business let's give it a name: Word Orgy. No explanation, that's its name. Maybe when you've tried it with different groups the name will be obvious. Or you can think of a more appropriate one.

The group/class is arranged into pairs. Each person should have one piece of paper and a pen. At the top of the page everyone writes a title, for example, 'Ford', 'Clock', 'Spider'. They then write a first line of six words. When each person has written a title and first line they swop papers with their partner. They read their partner's title and first line, and underneath write a second line, also of six words, following on from their partner's meaning. The pair then

7

swop again, and so continue, writing line by line about until they've got ten lines each.

There's only one rule, which is that they don't ask their partner to explain what he/she has written.

When the group have all finished their ten lines, the pairs swop papers once more so that each person has in front of them the paper with their own title and first line. Then it's time for everyone to read the piece to themselves. When that's established each person should be encouraged to read their piece aloud.

The purpose of this exercise? To begin with it's fun. But it also starts the words flowing. The usual pattern that emerges in the group is that for the first few lines there's a buzz of chatter and a skid of pens. Then as each piece progresses more concentration is called for to give the piece shape and/or direction.

There's a built-in snag. Each person has thought of a title and the first line. This most often means that they've begun to think of what they might write next. But no. The next line is written by their partner, who's got the same problem. When the paper is handed back to its original author there's more than likely a line written which is far wide of the author's worming idea. And now the author has to write a third line that relates to two lines, one of which isn't his. And so on.

The Word Orgy's presentation can be altered to suit many tastes. For instance, instead of the comparatively simple fare of six words a line, this could be changed to a syllabic count. Or a rhyme scheme. Or whatever other hedonistic variations are thought of.

How do 'nice guys win'? Co-operation. By leaving your partner with a conjunction at the end of your line, a friendly 'but' or 'and', 'because' or 'that'.

Equally it's possible to snarl up the line and leave your partner with a ringer to hang their brain on. Examples of these you can figure yourself if you're feeling that way.

Here are a couple of examples:

Pound Coin

A sparkling dot on the pavement
Trampled on by fifty dusty feet
Alone in a sea of grey pebbles
Is wanted by, noticed by no-one
But me. I stoop down slowly
And retrieve the smooth, round disc.
My curious fingers touch its form
And it slips into my pocket.
I look at the empty pavement
As my hand caresses the coin.

Evelyn Santer & Lyn Reeves,
St Bartholomew's School,
Newbury

The Big Oak Tree

Its trunk is as thick as a hundred men
And it's much, much bigger than Big Ben.
When the dark green leaves fall
They fall in my garden, over the wall
And when at night I talk under the tree
I'm really as scared as scared can be.

Jacqueline Hayhurst & Leanne Fyfe,
Park View County Junior School,
Basingstoke

I've found that the Word Orgy is a friendly way to set a number of people writing and I believe it's because of the co-operation element. If a partner starts putting words on paper and you know that they are soon going to be waiting for your contribution there's a sort of deadline urgency that sparks your brain. Add to that a natural curiosity to see what your partner has written, and your pen is provoked into action. Although the two examples are from pupils the

9

Word Orgy is something people of all ages can do and have done.

In the following poem the idea of co-operation is stretched to fit a wider canvass. During a workshop at St Mary's C of E Primary School, Banbury, Sue Stewart and I asked the children to write one line each for a group poem to be called 'Magic Island'. The title was then written in felt pen on a colossal piece of paper attached to the blackboard. When each child had written his or her line, it was added to the poem, sometimes with group discussion as to how a word or phrase might be changed for the better. In this way the children were able to grasp the beginning of the drafting process a poem might go through before reaching its final form. This is the draft poem which came out of that workshop:

Magic Island

I see a blue and red island far away
With crabs, spiders, pirates and sand,
Delicious cheeseburger trees, poppies
And daffodils. Dingbats and robots
Climb hills and coconut trees
To the din of pop music from the rocks.

There are bars, beams and a gym room,
Golden crisp trees, sausages and chips
On bushes. Among clouds and rainbows,
Apples make a special home for people.
There is a haunted house where witches live
And stars flash in the moonlight. Wizards
Shout, 'Morning is night, night morning!'

Lemonade rivers flow uphill.
Diamonds and rubies sprout in clumps,
Ten-pound notes grow on trees,
Unicorns dance and make magic dust.
Cotton wool and fizzy clouds
Make mountains of palm trees.
Oak trees whisper amongst themselves

And marvellous men turn to mice.

Gold sand drinks diamond cake,
Fairies prance like ballerinas.
I see a bluebird by a banana tree.
Robin and Batman's ship floods
Under water: hot sea, cold sea.

Rainbows in the bright sky
Plant toffee and balloons.
A sea of fish fingers drum the rocks.
Yellow moon and chocolate stars
Cover my magic island.

Another fruitful exercise in communal writing is the group riddle. This is to be done in groups of five. Each group decides on the subject of their riddle. Then each member of the group writes one line of the riddle, corresponding to one of the five senses. Then the group together writes the sixth line, which is to correspond with the sixth sense, or with the inexplicable.

Here are some riddles from a creative writing week tutored by Sue Stewart at The Small School, Hartland, Devon:

A speck of sun in the night
A damp fizzle
A smell of burning rises unnoticed
You reach forth to feel the small warm space
The taste must remain unsampled
Drawing people into its mellow atmosphere.

(Answer: candle)

Nick Church,
Mukti Mitchell,
Peter Dollimore,
Tim Medd & James Bonnefin

When opened you cry
For it has a hot temper

It wears many coats
It lives in silence
The pungent smell travels far
Some people like it, some not.

(Answer: onion)

Siobhan McCullough,
Hannah Rodway,
Carol Thorne,
Ines von Gerlach,
Polly Wheeler

A white cowpat ringed with spotless ladybirds
This cowpat smells nicer than normal
It tastes soft, milky and silky, unlike a cowpat
It feels like a cowpat, but touch isn't everything
And like a cowpat it's not very talkative
It's more desirable than the average cowpat.

(Answer: Strawberry Gateaux)

Simon Rodway,
Brendan Davey,
Andrew Dunne,
Sam Tithecott,
David Damon.

It's obvious that the solo writer staring at a piece of white paper isn't about to swop lines with a shadow (although that might be interesting) so what the individual can try is to pick a book – prose or verse – open it at random, pick a line or phrase and let word associations flow.

If after a few lines the barriers slam down pick another line and write whatever new associations you make ... be spontaneous. Going along with a wordflow, ideaflow, feelingflow can sometimes open floodgates of writing, at very least it is likely to reveal something to you.

I'm not suggesting that the writing produced will emerge

polished and crafted, but you could find you have ideas to fathom and word gymnastics to exercise.

Relish the Weird

... it cannot be denied that some valuable books are partially insane; some, mostly religious, partially inhuman; and very many tainted with morbidity and impotence. We do not loathe a masterpiece although we gird against its blemishes. We are not, above all, to look for faults, but merits.

Robert Louis Stevenson

I'd love to be able to define 'good writing'. Critics make their crusts from writing tomes on the merits of authors. Reviewers pan or praise books in a multitude of publications – the one you read is the opinion you receive. If there were a copperbottomed method to label 'good writing' the industrious critic and harassed reviewer would be looking elsewhere to process their words.

It seems to me that a piece of writing should be effective, by that I mean it should state what the author wants to say in the most effective manner and with language appropriate to what is being said. Because a book is a bestseller doesn't mean that it is going to pass the hardest test of all – that of time – and remain or become a 'classic'. The legends of authors whose books were turned down by all the major publishing houses, later to emerge (sometimes alas after the author has died) as hugely popular and highly praised books are well enough documented to warrant no more than a passing mention.

That we want to write is the beginning. That we have something we want to write is part of the process. That we have the words is essential. That we write them down is useful. THEN things start to hum, we learn that there are ways of putting words together that make them mean different things, tell us different things; the sounds they make have an effect and can enhance, or distract from, the meaning. So we learn to craft our sentences, we move words about until they are in the most effective relationship to one another, until they gell into the sense and meaning and sound we want to make.

I suppose an image that goes some way towards picturing what I mean is in a bunch of flowers. A person picks an armful of various flowers, grabs a container and plops them in. Okay they're flowers and they look pretty. But another person picks the same sorts of flowers then chooses a vase into which they arrange the display. I don't wish to labour the point but I suggest that the second way will be more effective. And even if no-one other than the person making the display sees what has been made the arranger will get satisfaction and pleasure from their effort.

The exercises that follow are quite a long way from picking flowers ... but they are a way to pick and choose among words.

Approaching ideas and objects from off-beat angles can give the creative writer stunningly weird sets of images. By looking at the commonplace and turning it upside down, or inside out, or seeing it through a distorting mirror, we give the obvious a fantastical effect. It's not necessary to break the rules of grammar, but if the rules are broken then provided the writer says exactly what he or she means then the weird can be full of wonder – and wonderful.

Here are some examples of the weird, or fantasy, put to good use:

On the Run

On your marks,
Get set,

BANG!

126 training shoes in couples
Start their jig.
They leap energetically
Across suburban paths.

The city air, unvirginal,
Caresses each lung
Leaving its black whore stains
On the clean pink lining.
Inside 73 stomachs muesli churns.
The oats and nuts bash each other
At every step and fail to fly
Quite as high as the raisins.
39 pairs of breasts
In all shapes and sizes
Bounce about like children on an inflatable.
34 jockstraps hold within
Sacred phallic flesh.

$25\frac{1}{2}$ miles later
126 training shoes
Cripple 126 feet.
Each step grates raw skin rawer.
73 stomachs have disappeared
And 73 husks run on.
39 pairs of breasts heavily sag.
34 jockstraps cling close to genitals.

$\frac{1}{2}$ mile later
73 people collapse
And regret their escape.

Lisa Pick,
Arvon Course at Lumb Bank

Names

A tree reaches from the upright trunk of t
Through the r's curved branches
And along the looping leaves of e's
Embodying its name.

A rock appears to work on the lump and strike
Off its own c and k.
All things take their names,

Greedily, as roots of oaks the ground.
But the name that names me isn't mine.

Phil Mitchell,
'Teachers as Writers' Course, Menai Centre,
Anglesey

Philosophy

If this is a poem,
Then this is a square –
    O
(It all depends on how you look at things!)

Stephen Earley,
Young Writers' Workshop,
Alderman Quilley School,
Eastleigh

In my introduction I mentioned that I was once given a blade of grass to write about. The challenge here is to write a verse or piece of prose taking as your subject (or object!) – NOTHING. This idea came out of a workshop given by John Moat at Braunton School, Devon. He'd asked the children to write a poem about a friend, and Nick Webber wrote a poem with gaps in it where the friend's name would have been. When John asked Nick what the friend's name was, he replied, 'His name's Nothing'. John asked him to fill in the gaps. This is what he wrote:

A Nothing

A small smelly Nothing is in Braunton.
It is $5\frac{1}{2}$ foot in height
And it is 110 pounds in weight
And it's a good thing
And I went and said to the Nothing
'What is your name?'
'It is Nothing,' he said to me.

17

And he said, 'What is your name?'
'It is Nick and I am a friend to you.
And will you be my friend too?'
'Yes,' he said, and me and Nothing
Went to the shop and Nothing said:
'I am your FRED.'

At later workshops, Sue Stewart used this poem to set children thinking along surreal lines. She read Nick's poem to them, without explanation, then asked them to write their own 'Nothing' poems, in whatever way they liked. Here are two examples from The Small School, Hartland:

I never see nothing
But I know he's there.
His breath is the wind
And the sky is his hair.
His body's the earth
And his blood is the sea.
I know and like nothing
Because nothing made me.
Nothing by Nature
Nothing by Name
God and Nothing
Are the same.

Peter Dollimore

NOTHING 1

O
it go
on to
hot tin hog
not init gin
thin Goth hint high
think thong thing
thought tonight
nothing

NOTHING 2

nothing out of nothing
no thin thing
no high tone
(note the additive:
'e' does not number in 'nothing')

if nothing hogs the hive
a lot has to go

Colin Hodgetts
Head Teacher.

Another word starter is to think of two or three people you know – they could be relatives or celebrities, politicians or historical characters – and describe them as a piece of furniture. To vary this exercise they could be likened to a meal, or an item of clothing, a house or a vessel, a city or village. And so on. Here are a few examples:

Dad is like a table top because he polishes his head.

Michael Fenn,
Park View County
Junior School,
Basingstoke

My brother is like a toaster as he is cold and plain outside, but warm and bright inside, and he keeps popping up when you least expect him to.

Sue Davies,
Castle School,
Taunton

My cousin is like a suitcase, open to everyone and always going places.

David Damon,
The Small School,
Hartland

My sister is like a book, all words no action.

James Bonnefin,
The Small School,
Hartland.

Riddles are a marvellous way to write about something or someone in such a way that the reader/listener is led to the name without the name being mentioned. We've seen the group riddle in Chapter I. Here are some individually written ones:

> I'm like a moon but I'm yellow and bright,
> I'm like a moon but you don't see me at night.
> There's a song about me wearing pyjamas,
> Frankly I'm bananas,
> What am I?

> I'm a fruit.
> I'm a gone wrong boot.
> I might be a U
> Maybe I'm new
> But maybe I'm old.
> What am I?
> (Answer: banana)

Adrian Bratt,
St Augustine's RC Primary School,
Weymouth

1. He hurries around, his surname is like a reed.
2. He sells meat, his first name rhymes with something you go across the sea on.
3. You have to get a lot into his name.
4. He built Paddington Station. His surname sounds a bit like a bear or a boxer.

(Answers: 1. Ian Rush 2. Terry Butcher 3. Steve Cram 4. Brunel)

Alastair Barrett,
Rhyme Roundabout,
Newbury Arts Workshop

To jump start the imagination and roar off into fantasy, try being wild with a number of 'Why is....' exercises: Why is soot black/snow white/ sky blue/ sun yellow/ grass green/blood red? Here are some examples from Park View County Junior School, Basingstoke:

Soot is black because smudge rolled in it.

Simon Hills

Snow is white because God was drawing snow and went wrong and all the rubbings went over the paper and burned it white.

Robert Jenkins

Sky is blue because when Coventry City beat Tottenham they were so proud that they threw their blue shirts in the air and they didn't come back down.

Stuart Hooker

Sun is yellow because when I went up in a hot air balloon I left my lemon squeezy on top of the sun and it fell over and spilt.

Michelle Lucas

Grass is green because God decided to put some green carpet in Heaven and it fell through the floor. There are gaps because he had it fitted around all the beds where the people sleep.

Leanne Fyfe

Blood is red because people ate too many beetroots.

Nicky Lemon

Essentials

What to put in and what to leave out; whether some particular fact be organically necessary or purely ornamental; whether, if it be purely ornamental, it may not weaken or obscure the general design; and finally, whether, if we decide to use it, we should do so grossly and notably, or in some conventional disguise: are questions of plastic style continually rearising.

Robert Louis Stevenson

I was told as a young poet that by naming things you invested a sentence with a particular power. Whether the piece you are writing calls for that particular power is a matter for the writer to choose.

The woman took her dog for a walk

or

Elizabeth took her corgi for a walk.

The first sentence is clear enough and says what it means but there is a certain amount of vagueness in it. On the other hand the second sentence tells the reader the name of the woman and the type of dog – brings the picture into closer focus – even opens up other connotations.

She picked a bunch of flowers

or

Elizabeth picked a bunch of snowdrops.

In the first of these sentences we are told what she's doing but nothing else. The second sentence tells us more. We know the name of the woman collecting the flowers. We are told the name of the plants she's picked. And because we also know that snowdrops appear in the early Spring we know the time of year. If Elizabeth had picked sweet peas the reader might well know that it was summer.

The point is that by stating the proper name of a thing

the writer can, if he or she wishes, give the reader more information.

The same works for verbs. There are many variations and degrees for an action, for instance TO SEE. We can spy, glimpse, glance, gaze, peer, and so on. We can skip, limp, stride, march, lollop – or we can walk.... These variations for a verb will, as for a noun, tell us more about the act. If a person limps down the road we know there is something the matter with them – it could be anything from a nail in their shoe to a twisted ankle or whatever. The verb TO LIMP indicates that the person is not merely walking. There is a condition to their movement.

Whether the writer wants to tell the reader these things is a matter of choice. An author decides what he or she wants the reader to know. And one thing the writer will most surely want is to dispel the Fog Factor. The Fog Factor is indicated by the amount of confusion there is in a sentence. But more on this later in the book.

I only want to introduce the FF here because, it seems to me, by giving things their names the writer clears the fog. The same applies with verbs; if the writer visualizes the act and condition of the act then he or she is likely to hit on the accurate verb.

The bane of the writer's life are adjectives and adverbs. For the beginner they are positively lethal.

Green pea. Blue sky. Beautiful house. And on and on and on. We really have to say to ourselves: 'Isn't there something more interesting I can say about a pea than that it's green?' So if every time an adjective latches on to a perfectly strong noun we ask whether something more interesting could be said, then we're beginning to write.

Verbs are strong. Adverbs on the whole are not. So, again when using an adverb, it is a good practice to query whether it is helping the verb.

Were the student writer to fine him or herself 10p for every adjective and adverb they used that wasn't fresh and invigorating, by the end of the month they'd probably have enough 10p's to buy....

23

Having said this I do not of course mean that the writer should avoid these two classes of words altogether. What I am emphasizing is that effective writing uses especially effective adjectives and adverbs. And those sparingly. When these words earn their places alongside nouns and verbs then they'll add grace and flavour to sentences.

Some examples:

Dear lady, I've become
a willow in your hand
who would prefer to be an oak.

Then I hear the name
and nature of that tree
as we whisper in the dark;

slow to mature, unmoving;
but willow may bend,
forever giving.

You took me at my word
last night, uprooted me
and stole my part.

I became heart wood
you an apple with the bond
of your forbidden fruit.

Terence Brick,
Newbery Arts Workshop

Wagtail on a Roof

Straight	Slate
Tapping	Tail
Grey	Bird
Blue	Roof
Flat	Slats
Fast	Strut
Quick	Claws
Tick	Tack
Slates	Dead

Feathers   Alive
It moves
They lay
Slates stay
Bird dies

Phil Mitchell,
'Teachers as Writers' Course,
Menai Centre,
Anglesey

Plas Newydd – A Photograph 1938

A footman perched on the wall
Uncomfortable in his uniform
Half smiles. At sixteen
His horizons, away from Plas Newydd,
Skim the straits.

He heard the curlew cry
He walked into the water's edge
He saw the clouds part
For sun to search the water.

Did my curlew cry for him?

Jane Lincoln,
'Teachers as Writers' Course,
Menai Centre,
Anglesey

Midnight Marriage

Every night the vixens cry
Every night the moon rides by
Tonight the moon is fast asleep
Tonight the vixens cannot weep.

Miss Lochelen
though dressed for bed
Miss Lochelen
is out to wed

25

Miss Lochelen
has banished the moon
for ...
Miss Lochelen
marries darkness soon.

Miss Lochelen
though dressed for bed
Miss Lochelen
is out to wed
Miss Lochelen
has banished the cries
for ...
Silence
Miss Lochelen's to bride.

Miss Lochelen
has her feet in mud
Miss Lochelen
has raven blood
Miss Lochelen
is lying down
but ...
Miss Lochelen
is above the ground.

Mrs Night
has her feet in mud
Mrs Night
has raven blood
Mrs Night
is up again
but ...
a shadow
is Miss Lochelen.

Emma Nugent,
Young Writers' Workshop,
Alderman Quilley School,
Eastleigh

Haiku

The tree lies dying
Rings show years on weathered bark
A fallen time-piece.

Kay Small,
Young Writers' Workshop,
Alderman Quilley School,
Eastleigh

When is a game not a game? When it's a sport ...? Here is definitely a game, good exercise too. It's word link, or word chain. Write a noun then follow it with the first verb that springs to mind. That's the easy warmer-upper. To make this word chain more interesting go on to associate noun-verb-noun. Make it so that the verb works for both nouns, for instance, Horse Jumps Fence or Athlete Breaks Record.

It makes sense for the words to have a recognisable association, although this game can be extended when the verbs are more quirky, less obvious. Then with other people to challenge the association of verb to noun it can be rewarding to hear how the relation is explained.

If one is searching for a reason for tumbling with the above wordplay then I think maybe the point of it has been missed; the exercise, as with most of the others in this book, is so that people wanting to write can feel free to bend and stretch their language until its muscles bulge.

When this type of exercise is allowed its head, writing dull or plastic phrases and sentences becomes a matter of choice rather than routine.

Art of Persuasion

Pattern and argument live in each other; and it is by the brevity, clearness, charm, or emphasis of the second, that we judge the strength and fitness of the first.

Robert Louis Stevenson

Have you ever wondered how objects, things, came by their names? Why is the ant called ant? Who first voiced that name for the little creature? Why is the mole called mole rather than something else? For me as they mountain my garden I call them furry JCB's. But I'm a long way behind. Mole they're called and mole they are. Unless ... unless they're a mark on one's skin, then they are altogether a different thing.

Putting a name to something must be a curious business. We all know that toddlers call things by names they can get their tongues around. But what about a new invention? When engineers (or whoever) came up with a grass cutter that had no wheels, no roller, just floated over the surface and cut the grass; where did the name Flymo come from, out of the recesses of whose brain? Why not Floatmo or Hovermo or Skimmo? With those three examples it's not hard to see why they weren't used. Then there's the floor suction cleaner. The name many of us use for the machine is Hoover and we even use that as a verb: 'I'll hoover the carpet'. Naming is important. And of course in business it's crucial. If a name catches on the product sells. Advertising copywriters dream up slogans to entice us to buy wares.

That's the obvious way to think of names. But as another thought, can a thing or object exist without a name? Without diving into metaphysics and tying our shoelaces together we've given ourselves that useful (and overused) word 'thing'.

'What is that thing?'

'It's a spoon,' says knowall.

There are people who sit at desks thinking of names for new fizzy drinks/face cream/perfumes/and anything else businesses wish to sell.

And it's at this stage this exercise comes in. Here's a list of unlikely items. Try writing advertising slogans aimed at specific outlets such as Afternoon TV, newspapers (decide *which* newspaper or paper), billboard/hoarding, magazines (again say which). There are many other places for slogans so there's no need to limit the choice of customer. Even children's comics are an outlet.

So with this word whirligig we 'Go to work on an adjective'. Glorious adjectives galore. Having up to this point put a shackle on adjectives we now binge on them. Reading the back of a cereal pack this morning I was saddened to read about a 'Special Offer' on a food mixer. I had hoped to read how the contents were Roasted, Toasted, Bursting with Sunshine and all that marvellous stuff. Give me the 'Snap Crackle and Pop' any day.

Before starting to write 'ads' for the unlikely items that follow, it would be an idea to collect three snappy slogans you've heard, read, or seen. Don't copy them!

If there's a group of people having a go at this 'starter' it can be fun for the 'ads' to be read aloud and the group to decide the best outlet for each other's slogans.

This exercise does concentrate the mind, and incidentally the choice of words. When we practise these 'starters' we're not aiming to write literature, the aim is to spin words and delight in using them. And, maybe, give others who hear them amusement.

1. Glassless windows
2. Wet Sundays
3. Holes in the road
4. Brakeless bikes

5. Rubber teeth
6. Perforated hot water bottles
7. Dishwater
8. Nonstick glue
9. Sandy sandwiches
10. Solid hinges
11. Invisible railway/bus timetables
12. Glass grass
13. Dentist drills
14. Mumps
15. Speaking taps
16. Confectionary telephones
17. Woollen knives
18. Rainbow steaks
19. Pageless books
20. Weeds
21. Nonstick stamps
22. Stringless guitars
23. Bristleless toothbrushes
24. Wickless candles
25. Broken elastic
26. Prison cells
27. Tinned snails
28. Slug soup
29. Thistle cake
30. Designer stubble
31. Interior decorating by Miss Havisham
32. The Flood
33. Sandpaper tissues
34. Mud carpets
35. Drain covers.

And how's this for 8-year-old James Honeyball's response:

> Tinned Snails
> Les escargots of the future:
> new tinned slow snails,
> and fastest slow meal.

Slug Soup
It's new and true,
don't go to,
eat it at a slug's pace.

Thistle Cake
The thorns tickle your teeth,
the flowers improve the colour
and the fluff gives you a quick clean.

Since this chapter is called the Art of Persuasion, and the title is meant to be taken lightly, here's another game to silver-word. Be a television critic for a day. Write a short pithy review of your favourite, then most unfavourite, television programme. Not more than two hundred words each. Here's the rub. Choose two of these publications and cast your review in the appropriate writing style:

Melody Maker
Woman
War Cry
Vogue
Financial Times
Health and Beauty.

If the T.V. review doesn't appeal write a report (again for one of these publications) on a historical event, preferably one long gone.

Cautionary tale:

The journalist is not reckoned an important officer; yet judge of the good he might do, the harm he does; judge of it by one instance only: that when we find two journals on the reverse sides of politics each, on the same day, openly garbling a piece of news for the interest of its own party, we smile at the discovery (no discovery now!) as over a good joke and pardonable stratagem. Lying so open is scarce lying, it is true; but one of the things that we profess to teach our young is a respect for truth; and I cannot think this

31

piece of education will be crowned with any great success, so long as some of us practise and the rest openly approve of public falsehood.

Robert Louis Stevenson.

Tune the Ear

Each phrase of each sentence, like an air or a recitative in music, should be so artfully compounded out of long and short, out of accented and unaccented, as to gratify the sensual ear. And of this the ear is the sole judge. It is impossible to lay down laws.

Robert Louis Stevenson

A word makes a sound when spoken. If we make an incomprehensible sound it doesn't do much – it may startle or soothe but it rarely makes a picture in the listener's head.

But across a room or a road a particular sound can have great effect and/or create a picture. So the sound of the word STOP can stop someone in their tracks. The sound of the word HOUSE will conjure in the hearer's head a picture of a house. I think there's something magic in being able to make sounds that travel through the air and make pictures in another's mind.

When writing, the sounds words make can help (or hinder) what is being written. Therefore it is useful to the writer to practise tuning words. It can help him or her work on a rhythm (or tune) to fit and enhance the sentence(s). A tune proper to one piece of writing can be hopeless for another.

To write: 'A bunch of grapes' is fine for one piece of writing; 'luscious clusters of the vine' is beautiful, one can almost taste the grapes in Marvel's poem.

Becoming aware of word rhythms is a beginning, practising writing to a rhythm is the next step.

Nursery rhyme with its emphatic tune accompanying the story is a good primer. Most of us know some nursery rhymes. For me they hold a special significance. As a child I recall being put to bed while a tune and some words of a nursery rhyme slipped around my head. I couldn't get them right, simply couldn't remember the lines. The tune I caught. I tossed and turned in my bed keeping myself awake until in the end I made up words of my own to fit the tune. Then I slept.

As a painter practises with colours and forms; as a musician practises with notes and chords; so a writer can practise with rhythms and rhymes.

It is difficult to write a sentence that doesn't carry some form of rhythm. It's a different matter altogether to maintain and use a rhythm throughout a piece of work. The choice of rhythm to coincide with what is being said is important: there is a huge difference between a languid summer day in a meadow and a frozen morning on the streets of a city. So the sounds words make should carry the meaning into the imagination.

The first exercise is to take a nursery rhyme and rewrite the words. Take a story from a newspaper or use a folk story.

Or choose a well-known song or ballad and rewrite the words to fit the tune, using an event that has occurred recently.

Another exercise that helps: make up a simple sentence in a staccato fashion, then change it to read in a slow, languid manner. For instance:

Hurt fades (staccato)

Pain cannot be fully remembered (slow).

These are exercises, so have fun with them. We're aiming to make our writing user-friendly.

Here are some examples of work showing rhyme, or rhythm, in action.

Making love to Wendy Cope

III

It was a dream I had last night;
Some sort of basis, and seemed a good title.

You're right, it's less of a poem,
More taking the Michael.

Ernie Wingeatt,
'Teachers as Writers' Course,
Menai Centre,
Anglesey

Dangling Man

This is the man who is dying to be dead,
Yet frightened, if he tried it, he might fail.
The winch waits, like a gallows, by the bed;
His legs lie broken, swollen, shining, pale.
The nurses come with cool, official eyes
Their voices warm in kind hypocrisy.
Can we, his children, counsel otherwise
Than swallow death in desperate ecstasy?
No chance. Defeated by a bottle top
His flaccid-fingered walnut-cracking hands
Twitch at his neck, pressing the pain to stop.
And is this what it means to be a man,
To watch my Father wrapped in swaddling bands
Swing like a donkey and die when he can?

Michael Jones,
'Teachers as Writers' Course,
Menai Centre,
Anglesey

Flute

The sound ripples, smooth on the calm sea,
hollow like a wooden pipe.
This flute hovers like a humming bird,
red and as light as afternoon tea.

Playing, it seems to tell of my emotions,
giving them away, these hidden secrets.

I can almost feel the composure
wrap itself around me like a warm blanket.

But the blanket is soon gone,
three red feathers fall. Instead,
a room is left, uncomfortable and awake.
The air is cold now.

Loud and quick it plays,
jumping, laughing, scorning.
Before, quietly it sang
its sweet Little Shepherd.

Rachel Hall,
Arvon Course at Totleigh Barton;
Castle School,
Taunton

Luthier

I set the sharpened plane and point
forward, work for a good rub joint
measured by sight.

The polished chisel, balanced arm
and the caution of skill charm
the dovetail tight.

The scraper quickens, burns my thumbs,
over beech till lustre becomes
hazed in the light.

I chip off amber glue, admire
the scent of cedar and the fire
of padauk, pay

close heed to the coats of varnish
with badger hair brush. I burnish,
then break away

from questions on the blue-print. I hitch
the strings, tune near to concert pitch,
run scales .... and play.

Terence Brick,
Arts Workshop,
Newbury
(Poem first published in *Prospice*)

Extract from Rosey's House

... Rosey's mother spent her evenings in the sitting-room, or,
if Rosey and I were installed there, in the warm kitchen where she
would sit at the table reading, or applying her formidably under-
used intellect to the Times crossword puzzle, taking off her apron
and putting on heavy spectacles for the event. The kitchen was
her territory, the source of warmth and comfort in the house, the
most used room, scene of innumerable meal-time debates and
noisy games.

Dominating the room was a black range which took up most
of one wall but which was used only as a fireplace, the cooking
being done on a shiny gas stove. Beneath the sash window stood
a solid chiffonier piled with books, maps, keys, crayons, diction-
aries, marbles, pens, pencils, schoolbooks, the jetsam of family
life. If you lifted off one of its doors (permanently broken, all it
lacked was a hinge) you would find it stuffed with a similar
miscellany of objects; railway timetables, board games, a dented
Bagatelle, playing cards and cricket bats.

If the kitchen was the warmest room in the house, its satellites
were the coldest. A sepulchral passage of scrubbed tiles led from
the kitchen to the scullery, passing the frosty marble-shelved
pantry where muslin-shrouded objects gave off a sharp cheesy
smell. At the end of the passage was the scullery, an almost
abandoned room containing nothing but an old enamel sink,
stained buckets and tangled mops. Above the door a row of coiled
springs with bells on gave rusty testimony to the passing of a more
affluent age.

Behind the scullery was the long garden and crumbling stable.
Adults told us the stable was dangerous, so we explored there

often. We imagined its attic was haunted, so we climbed up once out of daring, then left well alone. At various times in that garden we played tennis, rode our bikes furiously round the lawn, buried miscellaneous dead animals and later, at about the time that games gave way to sitting-room discussions, sat under the sycamore writing O-level essays ...

Leila Berry,
Arvon Course at Lumb
Bank

Making a piece of verse rhyme doesn't automatically mean that it'll have rhythm. And good prose carries a rhythm just as much as a well wrought poem.

The line in Leila Berry's extract from 'Rosey's House' that carries a subtle rhythm is: 'If the kitchen was the warmest room in the house, its satellites were the coldest.' There's a deft use of alliteration, the i(s) and the t(s) followed by r(s) working up to a climax of s(s). But of course the balance of the sentence has more in it than that, there's the image thrown in straight away of the kitchen (warm) followed by the splendid satellites, a marvellous image for somewhere or thing remote and cold.

Rachel Hall's line in 'Flute' that echoes a flute sound in my ear is 'This flute hovers like a humming bird,' with its alliterative f and v, h and u.

But don't let me leave anyone under the impression that by taking a sentence apart and reassembling it they will thereby understand its magic and might therefore be able to cast spells themselves. I'm glad it's not that simple. There's an unknowable factor, and that's hidden away in the head, heart and spirit of each writer.

Tight as the versifier may draw the knot of logic, yet for the ear he still leaves the tissue of the sentence floating somewhat loose. In prose, the sentence turns upon a pivot, nicely balanced, and fits into itself with an obtrusive neatness like a puzzle.

Robert Louis Stevenson

Invest Authority

The writer has the chance to stumble, by the way, on something pleasing, something interesting, something encouraging, were it only to a single reader. He will be unfortunate, indeed, if he suit no one. He has the chance, besides, to stumble on something that a dull person shall be able to comprehend; and for a dull person to have read anything and, for that once, comprehended it, makes a marking epoch in his education.

Robert Louis Stevenson

The short odds are that something we write is bound to be read by someone. Letters will be read by whoever receives them, a note for the milkperson – ugh, milkman will, we trust, be read and acted upon by him/her. With this latter 'note' what we want to write is information: 'No milk today, please'. Or whatever. A letter on the other hand enters more closely into creative writing. People often say to me at creative writing sessions that they find it relatively easy to write pages and pages to a friend, but snag on words when attempting a story or poem.

What seems to happen is that when penning a letter to an individual the writer has that person in mind and so pitches the words close to his/her 'voice', which the receiver will recognise. Check on the letters you receive from friends and note the difference between them. No two people write the same.

When it comes to a story or poem the world seems to intrude. (This is not, in my experience, a problem for children whose world is resolutely revolving around them ...) But the grown-up somehow hesitates and worries that what they write will be 'too personal', 'not up to much', 'uninteresting', and so on. To overcome this, few will gainsay, is hard. But there's always the exception. These we can let flow on and on and on.

For the lone writer (and writing is largely a lonely occupation) there are his or her notebooks which can be stashed away from prying eyes. In a creative writing group there should be a sensitivity among the members that allows anyone to opt out of showing or reading their writing. (It's curious that such sensitivity will often overcome a person's shyness/reticence.)

The modest aim of this book is to help the would-be writer to accept that playing with words can be both fun and serious. There's another avenue we should not ignore, and that is reading. Too often for my liking people I meet at creative writing sessions are woefully remiss with their reading. I don't mean 'The Reading List', although that's no bad thing, I mean just reading books for pleasure. For the writer, reading can be at least instructive and sometimes challenging. Instructive to see how the author has used his or her skill, and challenging when you read an author who has taken on and succeeded in pulling off memorable passages of verse or prose. Reading should not be neglected.

In this chapter I mention reading because I want to make a point about writing. When you read a book how many times do you skip the descriptive passages? No comment. But if the author writes descriptive passages so that every detail is exact and alive then the reader will savour the detail. By paying minute attention to detail, the creative writer can say all manner of things about a person or place. For instance, to give a reader a picture of two very different conditions of two women, he/she might devise a way that their handbags' contents were dropped on a table. Beside one fine leather bag there is a cheque book and Gucci purse, a slim gold lighter, car keys on a BMW ring, and so on. The other bag is faded plastic and beside it is a pension book, clear plastic purse with three 10p's, an NHS appointment card. Often the notion of someone having a good imagination is confused with their ability to 'see' detail. As a rider to this it needs to be said that the author may not

40

want his/her invented character to be given such close detail. So be it. When and how much detail to write at any time is the province of the author. To be aware of what intimate detail can do, whether it's about a plot of land or the contents of a person's bag or pockets, is a valuable part of the writer's craft.

Here are some exercises to try.

Describe in exquisite detail the following actions. To make these and other practises more telling, imagine that you're writing them to a reader who has no knowledge of the object you're describing:

1. setting a mouse-trap
2. lighting a coal fire
3. using a telephone to call a food-store and order goods for yourself for a weekend
4. putting an LP on a record player and playing it.

Or write a piece of prose, using short sentences, about:

1. a riot
2. a hot summer day
3. a morning jog/hike/swim
4. a favourite piece of music.

Or if you can, try to write a piece of verse on one of these themes. Or choose your own subject for the exercise. Remember to pack in as many details as possible.

Set out in front of a person a number of objects with the same name: i.e. glasses pencils shoes etc. Have one person then describe one of the objects until a listener can pick it out from its group.

You could grade the difficulty of this exercise by starting off with six glasses that are obviously dissimilar, for instance wine glass, tumbler, balloon glasses, spectacles. Then you can make it more difficult by putting glasses of a more related shape and size in the group. The same, of course, could be done with other objects.

And you can do this exercise on paper – writing the descriptions.

There is drama in detail. If you know that a man is in a dark, cobwebbed tunnel and has only one match, the tension is made. Bearing details in mind, write a description of/story about:

1. the felling of a tree
2. tea for two
3. being caught in a rainstorm in the open, a mile's walk from shelter
4. in a dentist's waiting-room
5. an engine misfiring
6. a feast.

Here are some examples of work showing detail in action:

Knitting in Pairs

Picking up green knitting needles
Which promised to soothe
Agatha chose fine angora
Remembering a long-dead twitching stare.
'Now,' she thought, 'for Sharon's V-neck.'
The pattern and texture excluded all thought
As shell-pink caught in scratchy fingers
And grew inexorably as time itself.
The clock ticked. No key turned the lock,
As love uncomplaining flowered.

Marion Gair,
'Teachers as Writers' Course,
Menai Centre,
Anglesey

Totleigh Barton

The blackbird drops to the lawn
And tug-o'-wars with stubborn worms.
The snowdrops shake their heads
To feel the morning's warmth.
The wall cocooned in moss
Sprouts bramble fronds and grass
Outlined by sun-shocked hills.
Rainwashed gateposts stand
Speckled with lichen

While in the fields March trees
Begin to green.
A breeze brings hints of spring,
The blackbird's voice is high on song.

Bridget Jones,
Arvon Course at Totleigh Barton;
Castle School,
Taunton

I'll Buy

If I could buy anything at all
I'd buy South Fork Ranch and Ewing Oil
Denver Carrington and Colby Co.
And the Queen Vic in Albert Square.

I'd buy St. Pauls and Buckingham Palace
And fly to France and buy the Eiffel Tower.
A piece of the world wouldn't be bad –
Brazil, Italy, Spain or Leningrad.

I'd buy all the banks, Midland to Lloyds
I'd buy all the shops from Oxfam to Harrods
I'd buy all the schools and change them around
I'd buy hundreds of dogs, how does that sound?

I'd buy industries coal to steel
I'd buy the Pacific and Atlantic Oceans
I'd buy a Mercedes, Porsch and Rolls
And I'd buy a set of Pyrex kitchen bowls.

I'd buy New York and Paris
For their splendour and wealth
I'd buy an automatic camera
And take pictures of myself.

I'd buy Wembley Stadium
And Wimbledon too,
North America
And a public loo.

43

I'd buy Australia and emigrate
I'd buy Russia to hibernate.
Before I start buying, there's one thing I missed out.
I'd buy a new pen 'cause this one's run out ...!

Fiona Doherty,
Edgbarrow School,
Crowthorne

Extract (Untitled)

When the only Piccadilly was in Manchester and all buses were red ... there must have been many other things which imaged unclear across the impressionable mind. The Lord was a shepherd she would not want and the 'His Master's Voice' gramophone kept on running down.

The aroma from the rice pudding, there in front of her, conjured up other smells; damp washing hanging from a wooden clothes horse; wet woollen jumpers pressed between sheets of newspaper, laid under the carpet to be trodden on and squeezed dry. These smells meant Monday; cold beef and boiled potatoes, and the inevitable row with Mr Robinson at number sixteen, who revelled in lighting smokey bonfires about noon of that day, to the chorused dismay of all the housewives.

Monday! Monday! Monday! Dinner money day!

A tattered plastic purse, holding a few personal items and two precious half crowns, would be opened and the money proffered. She never even noticed how scruffy the container, nor the fact that she was given its total contents.

'Don't lose it, keep it safe! Give it in right away!'

'Yes, mum.'

Off she would trundle, hand-me-down shirts, second-hand blazer and C & A imitation of the correct school skirt ...

... Returning home, she would encounter her mother's distractions. Heavily-laden purple lilac blossom; stems hammered, standing in cold stone jars, would fill the room with a perfume she could never forget. No lilac since had been as dark or as prolific; no stems as thick or limbs as laden. The room was filled

44

with clouds of scent and florets of beauty, releasing a headiness which drugged the mind into forgetfulness ...

Gerrie Shadwell,
'Teachers as Writers' Course,
Menai Centre,
Anglesey

I'd been working with a group of teachers for a few weeks when a new one joined up. I gave the teachers a choice of tempting titles to keep them writing while I saw individual people with the work they'd written during the week. The newly arrived teacher began to write. At the end of the session I asked the group to read out what they'd written that afternoon. When it came to the new one she asked to be passed. We went on. Next session she came late. I went over and gave her the day's title. She said she felt she couldn't write anything because the others had been so good last time. I took her out of earshot and more or less said what I've written in this chapter. I told her how important detail can be. Then I asked whether she'd recently visited her dentist. She had the day before, so I asked her to describe exactly and only what she saw from the chair. This she did, and anyone reading the piece would recognise those parts of the room visible from the reclining couch. The block was broken.

Visualize

... in all narration there is only one way to be clever, and that is to be exact. To be vivid is a secondary quality which must presuppose the first; for vividly to convey a wrong impression is only to make failure conspicuous.

Robert Louis Stevenson

Happily we all use our eyes in a different way. What is pleasing to one person may be dull to another. For the writer observation is important, whether he or she sees with the mind's eye or with the retina.

For this chapter I'm concentrating on the two eyes under our foreheads. It is seeing with our eyes that here concerns us. If two people walk down a street at the same time and at the same pace, and at the end of the walk are asked to write down five images that struck them, there is every likelihood they'll write different ones. I don't suppose this comes as much of a surprise because people usually focus on the things/shapes/happenings that most interest them.

On one occasion I asked two sixth formers for an image from the street outside the school. They went together. The girl's image was a tapestry dufflebag with red and gold angels embossed on it. The boy's was a Coca Cola can distorted by its reflection in a car hub cap. If you insist that gender played a part, so be it. I prefer to think it reflected their separate interest at the time.

The image, or picture made up of exactly chosen words, is a strong part of the writer's equipment. It acts as a most powerful launching platform for the reader's imagination. 'A painted ship upon a painted ocean.' That image of Coleridge's from *The Rime of the Ancient Mariner* is one

46

which sets me off on voyages that belie the seemingly still quality of the actual image.

Getting the picture right is a particular stroke of magic that as a writer one aims for: get it slightly off key and the whole thing falls flat. Mix up the images and it's like looking at a screen that has interference.

The exercise for this chapter couldn't be simpler. Find six striking images. Then write six pieces, each incorporating one of the images.

Another way of trying this teaser (if there's a group of people or a class) is for each person to write out on separate pieces of paper three images. Fold them up and put them in a hat, or somesuch, shake them, then let each person pick one out (or up to three). Should they pick their own images they can put them back and take others. The end result is that each person has someone else's 'found' image. Now write a piece – verse or prose – using what you've taken from the dip.

Or take a small plot of garden or room and write everything within that universe. Try taking a measure – say, three foot square – and make that your whole world. Don't just make a list of what is there but write it out as though you were visiting it as a stranger wanting to relate what is seen to a friend. Remember to name names. And be exact.

Some examples of imagery at work:

Moon Child

I am a night moth
in a white wind

I feel your eyes
on my moon-dress
my still dance
my face

half-mooned child
with Madonna smile
in the candle

in the crimson sand
behind black shrouds

I clutch
in wonder
an icon
and the sun
in clenched fist:

a porcelain vessel
smashed.

The blood
smears across my hand
from the ribbon at my waist

I stare.

I vanish.

Helena Michie,
International Writers Circle,
Cadaquez

Dad Dead

It always seemed a sketch,
An unfinished thing,
Like the interrupted swoop of a distant bird
As it perches clumsily on a top branch.

It was unfinished in the way of clumsy drawings,
Those of childhood
A worried density that, once, must have been
A stunning square of white
But became quickly smudged and rubbed
Into an inky thing of overworked intensity.

Each attempt to name and speak things unresolved
Instilled a lack of nerve ....
A top board diver,
Unable to step forward into space
The water deep a long way down.

And now no ear or voice
To hear or say
And their unfinished understanding left with him.

Phil Mitchell,
'Teachers as Writers' Course,
Menai Centre,
Anglesey

Watching the Sea at Bude

Pebbles site in wrinkled sand
Like buttons on an old armchair.
The angry sky is mirrored on the wet beach
And down by the water
Waves break in chorus-line kicks.
Gypsophila spray is tossed up to the wind
As the sea claps thunderous applause
On polished pebbles.

Justine Smith,
Arvon Course at Totleigh Barton;
Castle School,
Taunton

Haiku

An acorn so small
The old oak tree above all
Drops budding giants.

Andrea Legg-Bagg,
Young Writers' Workshop,
Alderman Quilley School,
Eastleigh

49

Postcard

An old man is out hunting
He's got a gun
His head is full of holes

Carol Pocock,
Park View County Junior School,
Basingstoke

Frogs

Bump, Bump, Bump,
Slime, Slime, Slime.
The frog emerges
As slimey as butter
In a frying pan
Splat, Splat, Splat.
He's lying on the road
Stretched to the fullest.

Tracy Mills,
Eton Wick C. E. Combined School,
Windsor

Monsterpiece and Flagstones

Below my feet, past tufts of thrift and purple clover and over and down, a single gull hang-glides on unseen currents and idly spans the deep chasm: a high doorstep to England that would repel the most intrepid invader. The cliffs of church-grey slate soar like a monsterpiece where great sea dragons might display their trophies, measure their time or prop their heels. Smashed on its sweeping slopes lie crumpled boulders, and beyond and beyond the vast translucent Atlantic Ocean, each green-blue wave a promise of another greener, bluer wave and another. Dark beneath the waves lie rocks, or are those patches cloud shadows? Wind on my face, sun on the nape of my neck, I lean on the wooden fence, finding security in the deep-dug post that presses into my back.

On my right a field of barley stands, ripe for the combine, its tricky roasted smell climbing into my nostrils. Beyond the church of St. Morwenna stands, tucked into a fold, tower peering over the trees like a startled rabbit. In the churchyard a tombstone, split by the root of a tree, declares itself SACRED TO THE MEMORY OF CHARLES TRICK, DIED 23rd APRIL, 1849 AGED 82 YEARS. MY LOVING WIFE SO DEAR ADIEU, LIKEWISE DEAR CHILDREN ALL, MAY YOU HAVE MADE YOUR PEACE WITH GOD WHEN HE FOR YOU MAY CALL. The church, a dark cave resonant with spirits, absorbs the sun and draws me in. Coolly confident, the pillars reassure me with their stability, and slate-grey flagstones torn from the cliffs, glossy with the passing feet of the faithful, lead me to the altar.

Freda Clark,
Arvon Course at Totleigh
Barton

Extract (Untitled)

This pomegranate rock smashed from a large boulder. The outer surfaces are blackened and rough; shark-skin to the touch. But the cracking of the mother stone has exposed a hidden beauty, the child's face. The grains are sharp, protecting an orange-speckled marble whiteness that light can touch. A leaden-weighted pomegranate lacking solidity. The striking of rock on rock is muted. Secret chambers steal the sound. I wonder about this piece because all around is a mass of the same rock. Enormous platforms of stone overhang the sheer drop to the valley bottom. Platforms angled back into the depth of the hillside like stanchions supporting some invisible bridge. Here are the same blackened surfaces, sometimes dull grey. The rock is split and a deep vertical crevice cuts into the heart of the stone. But that secret face remains hidden. The rock is a bloodsucker absorbing warmth from the early July sun. The stone remains cold.

The hill and its outcrops dominate the landscape. The spread of trees up the slopes has no chance. This is no lumbering whale with crustaceans holding fast to its skin. The trees are thin and withered as if the rock is absorbing goodness and spitting out the waste. Lush growth hugs the valley floor around the stream. Solitary stacks attached to abandoned mills still raise their heads above the canopy but they died long ago. Houses made of stone nestle among the trees but occupation can be only leasehold. There is a cave cut into the rock where the moss glows with a phosphorescent green. Outside, away from the rock, the moss is dull and insignificant; a stolen fleece. Rock stolen from the mother is abandoned and cannot be revived.

Even on this particular summer's day, when the valley floor is still, breezes gather around the hill-top as if their motion is governed by lines of force held by a lodestone lying at the heart of the rock.

There is power in the rock. And yet it is brittle.

David Terry,
Arvon Course at Lumb Bank

One thing to remember when you use a powerful image is that you don't want to hide it among loads of lesser images. If 'oak tree' is the central image then it's prudent to use other images that connect with the oak – acorn, branch, bow, root, leaf, twig and so on – rather than hare off into other picturesque images. To sum up. If you're using one telling image stick with it.

Escape from Cliché

This quote putting the cliché in the stocks is from H W
Fowler's *A Dictionary of Modern English Usage*: '... their
true use when they come into the writer's mind is as danger-
signals; he should take warning that when they suggest
themselves it is because what he is writing is bad stuff, or it
would not need such help; let him see to the substance of
his cake instead of decorating with sugarplums.'

When starting to write, clichés tend to abound, it is
therefore prudent to escape from them. They find their way
into pieces of writing because they come easily to hand. The
instant they slither from the pen the writer should beware;
has to send messages back to the brain for it to come up
with something fresh.

A useful way to break away from clichés is to take them
by the scruff and worry them out of existence. There are so
many hackneyed phrases available that it's hard to choose
ones for this exercise.

If there are a group of people then each person could
dream up and write down three clichés they find the most
abominable; hand them to another person who will
exchange theirs. Then write the phrase out of existence,
twist it, distort it, cast it into lead, or over a cliff.

The writer alone at his notebook can give him or herself
three of these warts and burn them out ...

Here are a few I find grating.

His/her better half
The psychological moment
The irony of fate
The cup that cheers
Any port in a storm

53

Too funny for words....

I'm beginning to get vertigo and am feeling *as sick as a dog*, so now it's up to you to pick your own and dispose of them.

... one rule is to be infinitely various; to interest, to disappoint, to surprise, and yet still to gratify; to be ever changing, as it were, the stitch, and yet still to give the effect of an ingenious neatness.

Robert Louis Stevenson

The examples that follow show how well these students wrote when they took clichés and used them as either title or theme, and deftly turned them to their advantage:

Pushy

If he was forty five
I was sixty two –
He wasn't half pushy.

In the middle of the evening he told me
Between the two of us we'd drunk twelve pounds.
I thought 'Oh, eck, it's one of them' –
Sent him off for two more gins.

There's some folks that are pushy
And some that aren't.

I told him I'd been out with three men
Since my husband passed away –
Not invited one in yet.

He came early on Saturday
I invited him in for an hour.
Well, I like them pushy.

Helen Baron,
Arvon Course at Lumb Bank

Bedsit

Take any room –
Create a womb, a tomb;
You have the choice
To vamp it up
  damp it down
  stamp your mark
Or to decamp.

You may tease in it,
    suspend it,
    freeze in it,
    lend it,
    sublet it
    (and regret it).

You can go to hell in it,
    reach the stars in it,
    lose your mind in it,
    free your soul in it,
    explode it.

Take any room ...

Judith Pollard,
Arvon Course at Lumb Bank

Extract from A Desirable Residence

Cycling behind Tom, Jane observed that his sweater gaped as he hunched over the handlebars. The stripe of flesh was white and doughy-looking. 'You'll catch a cold in your kidneys!' His head inflected, making his bike veer towards a tree. 'What?' She gestured that he should look where he was going.

The towpath took them past Turks Holiday Hire Cruisers and the Steadfast Cadet Corps, where two small, uniformed boys perched on the 'Steadfast Renown'. If Tom had a cold it would turn into a chesty cough and that would keep them both awake for nights. Gloomily, she pictured him propped against pillows, his coughs shaking the bed while she clung to the edge of her side,

55

counting the coughs in each spasm – two coughs, pause, five coughs at even intervals, then a final racking one – as regular as the notes of an irritating tune, reverberating through her body.

She worked her pedals hard to close the distance between them. 'Wait!' He wouldn't hear unless she yelled. She seemed to have to repeat everything lately. He said she mumbled. 'Well why should I have started mumbling suddenly? It's more likely that your ears need syringing.' Tom skirted a barking dog warily, giving her time to draw alongside. 'Be careful,' he warned her, 'you'll have me in the river.' 'I have neuralgia, I need to put on my hat.' She heard the stubbornness in her voice. Was she expecting challenge?

... A boat pulled past them. The oarsmen wore identical white shorts and vests with a blue stripe. Watching the disturbance of the water in their back-wash was exhilarating but it settled back too quickly to what it had been before. Tom was looking across to the opposite bank and his face had become suddenly animated. 'Just think, if we owned one of those houses over there, with private moorings, we could be on the river every weekend!'

Marilyn Sherwood,
Arvon Course at Lumb Bank

Clichés are invaders, they land where one least expects them. So it's sensible to keep your brain's radar alert and if the bleep of cliché appears, activate the red pencil and prepare the Tippex. Turn clichés round before they have a chance to take hold of your page.

Weave the Words

The beauty of the contents of a phrase, or of a sentence, depends implicitly upon alliteration and upon assonance. The vowel demands to be repeated; and both cry aloud to be perpetually varied.

Robert Louis Stevenson

The sound and the glory. Using alliteration or assonance effectively is not as straightforward as it may seem. Writing phrases and sentences using the same letter or vowel can create mouth-watering sounds but if the writer is not careful it can also cause a jaw-breaking mouthful for the reader.

Keeping control of key letters can limit the effect of a sentence, or it can give it extra verve and vibrance. The skill is in learning how to marry the letters or vowels you want to employ. It is no use turning out a sentence, or phrase, that lollops along languidly when it should, to carry its syntax, arrow its target. In that sentence I hope you can see and hear what I mean.

Before we crouch in our blocks to spring off with these exercises there's one other area of word-weave I want to mention; this is the sound-word. These are words that echo the sound of the object or act named. Cheep. Buzz. Hiss. Puff. Babble. Murmur. And so on. These words go under the general heading of onomatopeia, and can be useful to the writer.

Alliteration, assonance and onomatopeia can all be used together, as the following poem amply demonstrates:

Rhapsody in Brass

The sonnet of the cornet
And the warm yawn of the horn
Mingle unrhymingly
With the moan of the trombone
And the hum of the euphonium.

Stephen Earley,
Young Writers' Workshop,
Alderman Quilley School,
Eastleigh

Now to the starter. I call it the A to Z alliteration. The idea is to write a sentence for each letter of the alphabet, in order, keeping each sentence as closely alliterated as possible. To make this 'starter' more fun and challenging stick to a general theme. For example, use Food or Clothes or Characters.

Here is a piece of writing that developed from this exercise:

Cautionary Confections

Angie airs angular aniseed lozenges.
Bertram bursts bonbons by biting 'em through.
Chauncy is nonchalant, chawing on chewing gum.[1]
D'Arcy drawls, 'I devour dragees, I do.'[2]

Ermintrude errs, serves her After Eights early.
Fifi finds fruit spangles freshen furred tongue.
Googie is gauche, gobbles gobstoppers gawkily.
Hope holds that honey lumps help keep her young.

---

[1] Chaunc(e)y, a surname of French origin from a place name found in England from the thirteenth century, was the name of the second President of Harvard whose pupils used it for children whence it gradually came into use as a Christian name in the U.S.A.

[2] As well as our meaning of 'comfit', dragee has the meaning in French of 'small shot'. Avaler la dragee is to swallow the pill.

58

Ingrid is languid, spoons insipid ices.
Jake juggles jelly babes Jane judges rude.
Kirsty keeps kissing cascading flossed candy.
Lulu licks lollipops, lusciously lewd.

Marmaduke's marketing monogrammed marchpane.[3]
Nan nibbles tangerine slices: 'They're nice!'
Otto though ogles those whole ones in cointreau.
Prue proffers praline, exposing the price.

Queenie's quite queasy when quince drops are quoted.[4]
Refusing rum baba, Ralph rumbles, 'Replete.'
Sindy sips syllabub. Sandy sucks smarties.
Ted toys with Turkish Delight. Too effete!

Una unwraps universal assorted.[5]
Viv flaunts a vase of mauve fondants. His? Hers?
Walter's whipped whirls 're overweighty with walnuts.
Xavier exhales ex de luxest liqueurs.

Yolande is young, yearns for yellow-yoked creme eggs.
Yule logs at year-end; yields, yawning, to bed.
Zebedee, Zoe 'n Zaccariah are zealous:
Zell marzipan copies incised with a zed.

Joyce Maud Parker,
Arts Workshop,
Newbury

Or an A to Z of zany and not so zany headlines. This one from a 9-year-old at a workshop taken by Sue Stewart:

> Apollo 20A strikes disaster.
> Badger kills a man.
> Catherine Cookson plans to retire.
> Dragon's footprint 22 feet long.
> Elephants go mad.
> Figaro opera strikes top.

[3]'Per acumen ad lucem' – Trade Mark registration applied for.
[4]Compare the effect of apricocks on the Duchess of Malfi.
[5]The unwrappings are ubiquitous.

Gunman on the rampage.
Handel writes firework music.
Imogen stars in 'I want love'.
Jackson plans to retire after big hit single.
King Kong goes wild.
Lid goes for one thousand five hundred.
Mona Lisa stolen.
Never never land created anew.
On the moon families live.
Policeman killed by gunman.
Queen opens Parliament.
Roundabout breaks down.
Snake poison spreads.
Telly banned.
Una Stubbs the star.
Violet scent.
William Shakespeare relived.
Xmas comes early for hospital people.
Yak escapes.
Zodiac comes true.

Carys Ottner,
Rhyme Roundabout,
Newbury Arts Workshop

Or write a poem where the first letter of each line spells
out a name or phrase. This phrase is also the subject of the
poem:

Blocks of sheep
Always follow
After one another

Because that is how sheep are.
Alone in myth
Alive to fear

Beside a wolf a sheep
Lasts briefly.

Anciently flocked and
Cropped for wool sheep are
Kept in valleys to

Shorten sour grass. They also
Heap our language with
Enough droppings to
Explode this
Pictured verse.

This was written for a photo-montage made by the sculp-
tor Roger Leigh. It went on exhibition at the Photographers'
Gallery in London. An Acrostic (that's the proper name for
this type of writing) can spell out anything you want it to:
your own name, a place name, a refrain or nursery rhyme,
the poem's title.

Or try writing a piece of verse or prose about a long
night drive, using word-sounds (onomatopeia) to colour the
episode. Or a sea-journey. River-journey. Air-journey.

Some final examples show assonance, alliteration and
onomatopeia at work, to serious or comic effect:

A man wi a rabbit wi apologies ty Rabby (Robert Burns)

Try how he might
  He cudna dea it
The puir wee thing sey warm an' sleekit
Whut.
Tak it by its wee thin thrapple
And wi a twist its life tey throttle?
Och, How I wud if I cud, but I canny.
I wud if it was ma auld wife's granny.

John McCrum,
Arvon Course at Totleigh Barton;
Castle School,
Taunton

61

An Hour

Oak leaves whisper. Sycamores sigh. Insistent a blackbird. All the leaves in conversation. Insistent a blackbird. Beyond the leaves, water bubbles its way. Castanet train, brief, muffled. A tractor turning hay approaches, then turns. Blackbird persists. Gently roaring, miles above, a jet. The roar recedes and hollows. Yakkel of leaves increases. A frenzy of flies. Pin-sharp notes of an unseen bird, small, whose laser call zaps the glade. The leaves settle to sighing. A new bird, ack ack ack ack, ack ack ack ack. Above the leaves now a drone, increasing, above again the muffled roar of another jet. Still the drone lingers on, then is gone. Blackbird insists. Another, closer, joins. Now leaves jiggle. Oak leaves, busier, more keen to the breeze. The sycamore, serene, submits, but slowly. A distant blackbird's call. A heifer's trumpeting bellow. Urgent magpie prattles past. The flies return. Miles above another, gentler roar, hollowing. A brief cow-call. Leaves now at peace, just an easy weighing of branches. The quiet leaves allow the distant water. A castanet train, castanet train. Distant, a hollowing roar, and the wind, now fresher, hustles the leaves and grasses. It passes. Leaves around become still, and farther leaves rackle. A nearer dental drone climbs and fades. Blackbird insists. From behind, needle-notes. Blackbird insists. Needle-notes, still unseen, trill, spatter the greens. Another trill, a warble a trill and a trill. Blackbird persists.

John Stonehouse,
Arvon Course at Lumb Bank

I find myself easily convinced that the reason student writers seem to relish working with alliteration is because it's from the Anglo-Saxon taproot of our language. A glance at any large dictionary will show that our language absorbs words from many languages, nonetheless it is the strength and directness of Anglo-Saxon that sustains us.

While alliteration can be fun there's a warning that goes with it. Too much can sound awfully repetitive and sometimes frankly dull.

From the arrangement of according letters, which is altogether arabesque and sensual, up to the architecture of the elegant and pregnant sentence, which is a vigorous act of the pure intellect, there is scarce a faculty in man but has been exercised. We need not wonder, then, if perfect sentences are rare, and perfect pages rarer.

Robert Louis Stevenson.

Right or Wrong?

Thus any work of art, as it proceeds towards completion, too often – I had almost written always – loses in force and poignancy of main design. Our little air is swamped and dwarfed among hardly relevant orchestration; our little passionate story drowns in a deep sea of descriptive eloquence or slipshod talk.

Robert Louis Stevenson

There's white water ahead. Whether a piece of writing is wrong can have one skittering the canoe among waiting disaster. If the writer means to write a sentence or verse clearly and succinctly but, to his/her own standards, fails then he or she has probably got it wrong. If however the writer wishes to play with the Fog Factor and allow deviation and even a smidgen of confusion to hector the reader then a convoluted sentence, in verse or prose, may be exactly what the writer intended: they got it right.

How does the Fog Factor work? Use a scale of 0 to 10. If a sentence is accurate and has style it could score 0. If a sentence is difficult to fathom and falls all over itself so that at the end of it the reader hasn't the foggiest idea what the writer's blathering on about, then a Fog Factor of 10 or at best 9 is scored. Places where the FF might be found at its most dense are among official documents, the type that win annual gobbledegoop awards. Many of these go off the FF scale.

For the purpose of starting to write the Fog Factor should be applied to every sentence. As a warning a FF point should be awarded for each obvious adjective or adverb used. For anyone writing creatively it is best to write with the language we hear and speak. We are after all more alive to its cadences and nuances. So avoid archaic words and expressions. (These too score high rating on the FF scale.)

And it's not simply archaic words that can have us on the rocks.

Here are five examples of sentences that each carry a high Fog Factor:

1. The miniature canine jubilates to observe such jollity.
2. The feline squatted on the carpet.
3. Two minute marine animals, and a maternal marine animal as well, aqua-manoeuvered and aqua-manoeuvered all over the reservoir.
4. Incandesce, incandesce, diminutive stella.
5. All convivial personnel should congregate to assist the organised political group.

Each of the above is reasonably commonplace so I'm sure most people will be able to translate them to their originals. Try it.

Here are five more sentences which you can scramble into high Fog Factor:

1. Rain, rain, go away, come again another day.
2. My face is my fortune, sir, she said.
3. For men may come and men may go, but I go on for ever.
4. What shall we do with the drunken sailor early in the morning?
5. The quick brown fox jumps over the lazy dog.

The white water is there all the time we write, but we can blow away the Fog Factor. Or we can lessen it. See what you make of the following. When you've read it carefully and decided where the 'after all' might best fit, write a sentence yourself and place in it 'of course'. Then see whether those two words would fit anywhere else in the sentence, and if so, how would they alter the tuning of it?

So after all it would appear that I am able to do without milk.
So it after all would appear that I am able to do without milk.

So it would after all appear that I am able to do without milk.

So it would appear after all that I am able to do without milk.

So it would appear that after all I am able to do without milk.

So it would appear that I after all am able to do without milk.

So it would appear that I am after all able to do without milk.

So it would appear that I am able after all to do without milk.

So it would appear that I am able to after all do without milk.

So it would appear that I am able to do without milk after all.

Or try taking a list of commonplace things and writing them into different situations. See how they react. Do they come alive? Are they more or less dramatic/comic/visual? i.e. a clown has his own image. Take that image and distort it. Have him out of place, out of context (on a bus, on a pylon), or have him do things unusual to him (go shopping, feed the ducks). Then write a piece of the same length putting the clown back in his proper place. Compare the two and see why the first doesn't work. Or if it does why it does so.

Do the same with: A Bank   A Law Court   A Cup   A Rose. Or any other object that triggers your imagination.

Arvon

Typewriters
Yattering
The knocking knees of uncertain progress

John Stonehouse,
Arvon Course at Lumb Bank

Imaginative Tales

Now the first merit which attracts in the pages of a good writer, or the talk of a brilliant conversationalist, is the apt choice and contrast of the words employed. It is, indeed, a strange art to take these blocks, rudely conceived for the purpose of the market or the bar, and by tact of application touch them to the finest meanings and distinctions, restore to them their primal energy, wittily shift them to another issue, or make of them a drum to rouse the passions.

Robert Louis Stevenson

We pay lip service to our oral tradition but do very little to support it. Although there are, I'm glad to say, people who are actively, through workshops and at festivals and such like, keeping the tradition alive. To them we owe a debt. Maybe the best way to pay that debt is to take story telling more seriously.

It may seem odd that in a creative writing book I should advocate story telling. But one is closely related to the other.

How many times have you heard or read that a novelist is a good story teller, weaves a good yarn? The narrative poem (so long out of fashion) is one of the earliest forms of poetry we have. And there's a reawakening of that tradition among contemporary poets.

In much the same way as the writer can be daunted by the blank page, so a person may become tongue tied if asked to tell a story. I don't mean the practised story teller. The people I am addressing are those of us who sometimes or rarely string more than six sentences together when we speak. You will probably notice that most conversations are conducted in short, even unfinished sentences. Conversation is different from story telling. The prime and most common story is when something has happened to a person, or they've seen something out of the ordinary and they can't wait to relate this event to someone, preferably a friend or relative. A simple example might be witnessing a fireman rescuing a kitten from a tall, flimsy tree. The novice story teller will blurt it out: 'In the park I saw a fireman climb a tree to get a kitten that was stuck.' Okay that says it but it's not rivetting. An accomplished story teller will prepare the listener, settle them. You know the sort of thing. 'Are you sitting comfortably ...!' This story teller will lead you into the park, tell you the time of day and what the weather was like. You'll be held by details such as the name of the tree, what the fireman was like, and the state of the kitten. He/she may well end the story with the reaction of the crowd, or the reaction from the owner of the kitten, or how the fireman or kitten acted once on the ground. The details keep the juices of the story flowing.

Anyone can tell a story. Children adore being told stories, as many parents know.

Story telling is a good exercise in use of language. As such, at least, it should be encouraged. One of the ways to begin is to suggest to your group or class that each takes a story they know and then retells it in their own words.

Children might retell a fairy story or nursery rhyme as though it was happening today. Providing they are confident that they know the plot, their imaginations and language can fly. I've heard some incredible retellings of Jack and Jill, and even Hickory Dickory Dock. In the latter, the most extraordinary story by a primary schoolgirl turned the mouse into a spaceman and the clock into the moon. It ended up with the moon kicking the spaceman off at exactly twelve o'clock.

I doubt if it will come as a surprise when I say that for adults story telling can sometimes be hard. As with writing, this often stems from the prospect of getting egg on the face. Tensing up. Being afraid to 'make a fool of oneself'. This is an entirely understandable attitude but if it is overcome the gates can open to confidence with language and delight in words. It is important not to set hard and fast rules. And certainly not to make it law that everyone MUST tell a story. The more strictures there are, the more closed and silent are the lips.

However, with a group (or just two of you) stories can emerge. Again the starting point can be straightforward. Take a well-known story or event or piece of history – whatever, and retell it. The dateline can be changed, the characters might take on different characteristics, even the plot might twist and turn in a new way. Or, of course, the story could be told faithfully. And the thing about this is that because the story or event is being related by someone other than the originator, it will inevitably change. It will in some way become another story.

The ways of telling stories are as many as the ways of writing them. Which is merely another way of saying that each person brings to the oral or written piece their own 'voice'. And we should all be grateful for that.

Having fun with language is a serious business. The flexing of the imagination, and the way in which we keep to the essence of what is being said or written, is a skill that requires attention and active involvement. To live, a language must develop. It must grow with the spirit and needs of the time. It must accommodate the entire gamut of people's expression for the world, or the part of it they inhabit. Right now our language is extremely powerful internationally. But we should not forget that its prime function is to allow those who speak and write it to communicate as best they can – across generations as well as across oceans.

An afterthought and anecdote about story telling. At a Christmas gathering with friends, a girl confessed that she didn't know Dickens' Christmas Carol. Across the room sat a friend of mine sipping wine. I went over and suggested to him (he's a collector of Orkney stories) that between us we 'Skat' told the Christmas Carol for the girl. This is when one person starts a story, then stops along the way for the other to take it up. Then the second person stops and the first picks up the threads. And so on, until the story is told. Dickens just might have recognised his marvellous story. The girl when we'd finished said that she'd go away and read the original. That was good enough for us.

A lovely idea has been sent to me by Philip Toogood, Head at Dame Catherine's School, Derby. This is what he had his pupils do:

'Stage (1) Older student interviewed younger student about what story line was in younger person's mind.

(2) Older students met as a group with me and retold orally the stories round the table (hilarious).

(3) Older students wrote out story and tried it out on younger students, following this with amendments and corrections.

(4) Older students word processed stories ready for:

(5) (next term)
Younger students to illustrate stories which will then be pasted up and put together as a little booklet.'

And here is an extract from a story that developed from this exercise. We pick up the threads after Henry Shuffle-bottom has made a garden with his new spade, given to him by his son for his 47th birthday. After discovering 47 gold bars under the soil, which he promptly spent, he and his wife Sarah become greedy:

What A Find!
Charlotte's Story, by Jadie

So out they went and dug for more gold. Dig, dig, dig, went the spade. But all of a sudden came an EEEEEEEEEEEEEEEEEEEEEEEEEK! And then another EEEEEEEEEEEEEEEEEEEEEEEEEK!

Henry dug further and discovered three tiny people. 'Sarah! Come here quickly!' he shouted in amazement.

When Sarah saw the three tiny people she too gave a quick EEEEEK! and nearly jumped out of her new six-inch yellow plastic stillettoes which she had bought for gardening and general knocking around! Henry asked the three little people their names.

The one girl was called Yellow. She was three years old and had lovely pink long curly hair. The second one was a boy. He was called Nottingham and was five. He was wearing the funniest clothes imaginable, funny black shorts and the most ghastly purple jumper. The last boy was called Grass and was a bit dopey ... for saying he was seven years old. He had short brown hair and wore an orange T-shirt.

Henry asked Sarah what they should do with the tiny people. She suggested they should put them in a jam jar and then cook them in the microwave. So of course Henry agreed that that was the answer.

They put them in a jam jar for 8 days and then cooked them. They had them for their Sunday dinner and had a real feast. They both looked at each other with faces and bellies bulging and they both knew what each other was thinking. They wished that they could have some more! Because they were that nice. But ... but ... but ... BANG!

They both EXPLODED.

... and that's what happens to greedy and mean people.

Jadie Wardle &
Charlotte Gavin-Jones

The following tales have been around for many years. Where it was I first heard them, I've long since forgotten. They probably have undergone the inevitable addition and omission that stories undergo after much telling.

When you've read them ask yourself, could it be that I have not ended each fable? You might try a further conclusion to each one.

1. A Mediaeval Minstrel

This poet left his home to undertake a reading (singing) tour of the great Halls and Manors of the north. He had a thoroughbred horse of which he was especially proud. To fool the footpads and ruffians on the road he always dressed in old clothes and cloak and covered his good horse in mud.

He also made sure that his sword was well goose-greased for easy draw (not that he was more than an ordinary swordsman). Anyway he avoided trouble on the road and completed many successful stops. He made a good sum of money, being paid a groat for each Fit or stanza of ballads that his hosts enjoyed.

Having finished his tour he headed home with saddlebags ajingle. On the return road he was mugged. He was clubbed and left in a ditch. His bags were taken. Because his horse was travel-worn it was ignored, so he dragged himself into the saddle and made for the nearest Shire-reeve (sheriff) and told of his misfortune. He complained that he'd been robbed of an amount of money. They listened with sympathy. Then asked him how he came by the cash. When he told them he was a minstrel, a poet, they looked puzzled and doubtful. How could a poet earn any money they wondered. However, they said they'd look into the matter and see if they could catch the villains. And dismissed him. He rode home penniless.

2. Magical Poet

A poet, being ignored and neglected and scorned by people who had thought they would like to be entertained and amused by him, wrote a magical spell on the dust of a table in the house as he left.

When one of the people opened the door the dust flew all about, causing the spell to spread and alight on those who had insulted the poet. They broke out in red blotches.

The people swore and scratched and cursed and tried all known remedies to get rid of their irritations.

Later one of the people found a note pinned to an outside door telling them that if they tried with honour, wit, and appropriate rewards to understand the work of the poet he would reverse the spell.

3. An Oriental Poet

This poet gave up an easy government post and went with his wife to live in a remote house miles from anywhere.

72

There for many years they lived, eking out a living as best they could.

One day when the pressure had become too much the wife turned to the poet and told him that they must have some money to renew things and buy food. As it happened a poetry competition was proclaimed carrying a large cash prize. The poet entered a poem. And to his wife's delight and his own surprise, he won.

His wife gave him a shopping list and he set off to collect his prize. On the way he passed a pottery. The master potter had just finished a special pot which he displayed outside his workshop. The poet looked at the pot and thought it the most wondrous thing he'd seen. He went in and asked how much the pot cost. It was exactly the amount he'd won. The poet collected his money, went back to the potter and bought the pot.

And how about these two examples to show how different one storyteller's 'voice' can be from another:

Whatever Happened to the English Rose?

Frankly Madeline I don't know why I allow myself to be taken advantage of so ... Ronnie's a sweet man, but really if he can't get Higgins to stop breathing garlic fumes I shall have to deal with it myself.

Quite Miss Winter-Wright ... could I suggest, one slight alteration – perhaps the dress, a little more on the shoulder?

My dear girl one must emphasise one's assets, my bust was once sculptured don't you know, up and coming he was, made quite a name for himself I hear. If only you took a little more pride in yourself Madeline, this natural English rose look is all very well under thirty dear but perhaps if you pushed yourself forward men would notice.

Miss Winter-Wright this is your quarter of an hour call.

Lace my boots there's a good girl – nice and tight, such pretty feet. 'A ravishing and delightfully buxom Elisa' – that was this morning's, it'll please Ronnie of course. Can't wait to get back to town though, time does drag in the provinces.

Small rent in the back Miss Winter-Wright, just a trifle – must be inferior material.

Take a tip from me: beauty is from the inside – believe in yourself – by the way that delightful husband of yours told me you played Ophelia once, seemed quite proud of it – said sweet things about my performance – quite a charming man isn't he?

This is your call Miss Winter-Wright.

That's why the audiences love me Madeline – I believe in myself. Have my change ready nice and early won't you dear?

Madeline that intolerable man dropped a line again, I'm sure he drinks; so unprofessional; well I wasn't going to help him out.

Your shawl Miss Winter-Wright, slightly soiled.

Is that absolutely necessary? Ronnie has some quaintly strange ideas – never mind Madeline it barely shows. Pity you didn't make it – quite pretty underneath that hair – off your forehead I think – expose the features, that husband of yours cuts a dashing figure, most attractive too – so nice to find a perceptive man – thought they didn't exist out of town. Of course Ronnie adores me – he really is rather limited though, sweet; needs guidance. You must tell me about your little Ophelia one day dear, perhaps I could help you. Terrible career though, so demanding. Love it though, couldn't conceive another life.

May I attend . . . your dress? perhaps those top buttons fastened . . .

Now Madeline don't interfere – Ronnie's just a little tense about it all; he's very young, lacks experience of course, that's why I stay – the offers I've turned down – you wouldn't believe it. The silver taffeta for the party tonight Madeline and a rose I think, pinned to the breast, just adds a touch of excitement to the sophistication make sure you're here on time; I shall need you late tonight. Oh, and Madeline – keep yourself in the background dear – you don't want to appear pushy.

Helen Elliott,
Arvon Course at
Totleigh Barton;
Castle School,
Taunton

74

Extract (Untitled)

... The week was nearly over and Norman felt stifled. All the blinds in the street were tightly closed as was Mrs Collins' front door for the first time in Norman's memory. To shut that door was a sign of unneighbourliness which no-one in the street ever risked. But today was different.

'We can have a game of marbles,' Kathleen had suggested. 'Marbles!' he had protested, with an outraged sense of their unseasonable nature, but Kathleen with all her little motherly patience had explained their alleys would be quieter in the gutter than her pram clattering along the flags.

'She's dead,' informed Kathleen.

'Yes, she's gone,' muttered Norman uncomprehendingly. He squatted on the pavement edge looking at the tightly wired wreaths piled against the wall on Mrs Collins' yellow flags. He knew that it was his mother who had early that morning renewed the rubbing stone 'as a mark of respect'.

'Eh look!' Kathleen nudged Norman, pointing upwards to the bedroom window where he could see those men who only a few minutes earlier had solemnly trooped black coated into the house, now in their shirtsleeves. They were struggling with that window. Soon both panes were out of their frame and news of these activities had mysteriously spread. Women edged silently out of their darkened houses. Kids from other streets joined Norman and Kathleen, uncaringly smudging the yellow flagstones.

Suddenly, ropes snaked out through the open gap in the wall, and the dark mahogany shape of a coffin nudged after them. Only Norman understood what was happening. It had always puzzled him how that mountainous flesh had squeezed up the narrow stairs when she was alive but it was certain that she could not get down them now she was dead ...

Gordon Graham,
'Teachers as Writers' Course,
Menai Centre,
Anglesey

It's not unheard of for me to contradict myself. At the beginning of this chapter I said that conversation is different from story telling. Yes it is, but recalling some of the accomplished conversationalists who've enthralled me I remember that their conversations were often peppered with stories and anecdotes. So perhaps the paddling pool for story telling is in conversation.

Tempting Titles

Now this spirit in which a subject is regarded, important in all kinds of literary work, becomes all-important in works of fiction, meditation, or rhapsody; for there it not only colours but itself chooses the facts; not only modifies but shapes the work. And hence, over the far larger proportion of the field of literature, the health or disease of the writer's mind or momentary humour forms not only the leading feature of his work, but is, at bottom, the only thing he can communicate to others.

Robert Louis Stevenson

Nevertheless, to have something to write about is as essential to the student as is having a pen with which to write. Recently I was talking to a 'scene of crime' detective who told me that when he joined the Force he and the other recruits were told to write an essay on either 'Why I Want to be a Policeman' or 'The Best Holiday I Ever Had'. Neither title inspired him, he thought the first too dull and likely to lead him to say the obvious or else he might write something that could snag him during later interviews. So he chose the holiday. He said that he felt on safer ground because he could write more freely. He could allow himself more scope with the language without having to worry too much about his reader(s) probing the context of his essay.

For some writers, arriving at a good title is like panning for gold in the desert. I know of one poet who bought rolls of white ceiling paper and scrawled titles on them with a large felt-tip pen. It used to hang from the wall of his workroom so he could decide whether to accept one or more of the titles he had written.

In a creative writing situation the title has a different

function. It acts as a pump primer, it gives the student writer the opportunity to start the words running.

I've found over a period of time, and with many and varied groups and age ranges, that the most effective titles are those which point towards a storyline. Then add a soupçon of the surreal so each individual can choose a starter that suits his or her twist of imagination.

Most creative writing sessions take place over a limited time, usually one and a half to two hours. When working within this schedule it's sensible to suggest an approximate length for the piece of writing: say, a maximum of two pages of A4. I think it is important that there is enough time for students to be able to read over what they've written, redrafting wherever necessary, and read aloud the work done. The time scale will naturally vary depending on the size of the group/class and the number of persons involved.

Should the number be large, say twenty or so, and the time short, then the 'Mini Saga' is a splendid idea. I believe this was thought up by a BBC radio presenter. The discipline is to write your story in *exactly* 50 words.

The titles that follow are ones that I've suggested over several years to creative writing groups and at schools. They are meant, for the most part, to give students the chance to have fun. What is curious about using titles such as these is that because they are accessible, weird, unpretentious, they seem naturally to coax the student into a free-flow of words and ideas.

Once students have broken the barrier of the blank page, and begun to play with words and rough it out with them, there's a whole growing process that can lead to individual achievements – completed stories and poems.

By no elastic of the imagination is it suggested that everyone who participates in creative writing will, ipso facto, turn into a published writer. In my experience this is not the overriding motive of most students. Some yes, but not, I think, the majority. Nonetheless learning to express oneself, understanding the power of effective use of language, and seeing how crafted writing can move, enlighten and delight, is in itself an achievement.

I've been told by writing students, who have no intention of publishing anything they've written, that the bonus they gained from creative writing sessions was the difference it made to their reading. They say their reading became richer, deeper and more selective.

There is nothing sacrosanct about these titles. I wrote them down for diverse groups over a period of time. They might be used as they are or they can be adapted to suit a particular session or occasion. I've found that even when several students pick the same title (though this is unusual) the pieces they write will, by the uniqueness of the individual use of language, be very different.

Titles or Themes

A Plea for Dragons
Letter from Mrs Beaton to Miss Havisham
Last Will and Testament of Toad of Toad Hall
10 Questions Mensa Cannot Answer
Job Description For a Galley Slave
Why Humpty Dumpty Joined BUPA
The Other Side of Nowhere
The Psychic Warrior
The Problem is the Problem
10 New Insults, 10 New Compliments
DHSS Quiz Snow White on her Domestic Status viz-a-viz 7 Dwarfs
Grethel Explains Feminism to Hansel
Goliath Tells His Side of the Story
Day in the Life of a Hedonist
Genghis Khan's School Report
Social Service Report on the Old Woman Who Lived in a Shoe
Toby Orre Knott Toby
Club Rules for a Chaingang
'It's so disarming' by Venus de Milo

Walter Mitty Visits his Analyst
Salome Takes Dancing Lessons
Recipe for a Disastrous Xmas
Retell Red Riding Hood as though it Happened Today
Write Minutes of a Meeting of The Round Table at Camelot – AOB by Merlin
Accountant Considers The Charge of The Light Brigade
Fagan's Proposal for a GCSE Course
Write a Reference for Someone to Become a Skydiver
10 Reasons for Doing Nothing
The Proper Use of Confusion
What Would Happen If: Eve Ignored the Snake. The Wheel Wasn't Invented. We All Understood Each Other.
The Gnomes' Revenge
Ivan The Terrible Writes to his Mother
St George About His Demotion
Masterful Inactivity
North of Midnight
The Tribe That Saw Tomorrow
A Plea of Mitigation by Oedipus
Jonah Consults a Travel Agent
Blurb for a Holiday on the Ark
The Tooth-Fairy Joins the NHS
Sherlock Holmes Buys a Second-Hand Car
It's All Swings and Roundabouts
Man Friday's Story
I Enjoy My Phobia
Helen Launches the 1001st Ship
At The Edge of Forever
Christopher Columbus Visits Broadway
It's a Promise
Joseph's Tailor's story
Found. The First Drafts of the Commandments
My Day by Lady Godiva
Surveyor's Report on the Tower of Pisa
Just William's Wedding

Vice Squad Raid Teddy Bears Picnic
Out in the Fast Lane.

Another challenge is to write a Haiku (a three-line poem with 5 syllables in the first line, 7 in the second, 5 in the third). This makes you think carefully about the words you choose, especially when tackling cosmic titles such as:

Moby Dick
The History of the World
The Fall
Marriage
The Great Wall of China
The Sky at Night
Acid Rain
The Wheel
Fire
A Circle
Time
White.

The following pieces of work originated from the tempting titles above:

Extract from A Charge to the Light Brigade

I like to think I owed my promotion to lateral thinking, but basically I suppose I really had Lord Cardigan to thank. He'd called in our firm of management consultants with a broad brief to cut costs and improve efficiency.

So here I was in the Crimea after disembarking at Odessa and travelling overland to Sebastopol where I'd met Cardigan and his cronies.

Well the problem was easy to see. There was rampant over-manning and at 3d per day for each person the bills were mounting rapidly. Lord Raglan put up a feeble argument that we needed these people – soldiers I believe they're called – to fight the Russians or Prussians or whatever. However that's hardly an excuse I can bring back to a head office that's down to its last butler is it? The trouble with overmanning of course is not only the assets employed to return on capital ratio but the ongoing commitment with pensions and all that other socialist nonsense like free hospital care. If BUPA's good enough for me it's good enough for Florence Nightingale.

One way I managed to reduce costs at a stroke was by insisting that ammunition could only be used every other day. That was creative thinking of the first order I felt, but I was circumvented by Raglan who made an agreement with his opposite number that they would only fight on Monday, Wednesday and Friday. That suited his opposite number no doubt, their factories were so damned inefficient they probably couldn't produce the ammunition in the first place. Use bayonets, I instructed Raglan and his henchman Lucan, cheap, last longer and provide jobs in Sheffield where my uncle just happens to own a steel factory.

I also got rid of those heavy greatcoats and solved two problems at once. Those things cost 9d a time would you believe, and impeded movement so much that their sale not only realised a useful cash sum but forced our men to move quicker in order to keep warm, thereby saving on logs for the fires.

Now every self-respecting management consultant will tell you that horses are bad news. And this outfit had 600 of the things! I don't know what their accountants could have been up to, allowing the capital expenditure for that. Of course the horses had to go, although no other army with a halfway decent management consultant advising them is going to actually want to buy them. Raglan again (what a pain that man is) argued that you can't have a cavalry without them. Outdated thinking like that should have no place in a cost conscious modern army, and I can see further resistance from him should I try to get rid of these soldier people running around all over the place ...

Tony Brown,
Newbury Arts Workshop

Roundabout MacNiece

It's all swings and roundabouts:
You're taken for a ride.
It lasts until the music stops
And then you step aside.

It's all aboard to kick the sky:
Which boat's for sailing highest.
It's chance a hunch or cast the die
But keep your powder driest.

It's all a turn at pitch and toss:
Whose penny rolls the straightest.
The earliest bites the cherry first;
The stone awaits the latest.

It's all a hall of mirrors jaunt
Or tour a house that's haunted.
It's winning what you didn't want
Or losing what you wanted.

It's all a shy at coconuts;
It's goldfish short of water;
Or bowling for a squealing pig.
The laughter spells the slaughter.

It's all a helter-skelter glide
With thrills and spills in waiting.
Fine lines divide; they're side by side,
The loving and the hating.

It's all a sinuous switchback course
With down and up momentum.
It's suss the system's tour de force
And make rules serve or bend 'em.

It's all a romp at dodgem cars
Where coolest nerve is strongest;
Who corners fast can bumper last
And who bumps last laughs longest.

It's all a cambered circuit race
With wagers on the drivers;
Who gains a lane can push the pace.
It's make or break the fivers.

It's all a scenic railway whirl
Come fair or stormy weather.
Sit tight to watch the world unfurl
And we'll go round together.

Joyce Maud Parker,
Arts Workshop,
Newbury

A Promise

I hear a voice proclaim
as you feather my brow:
'Make her a promise
you can keep.'

My arm reverts
the vacant room
and my heart floats,
a cypress leaf
in a midnight well.

The liquid moon
I hope to fetch
from its darkness;
but I could drown
in your green embrace
lichen-clad and moist.

So, refine me
to a bright shore
where the auburn sun
engulfs the grape.

Then I will cast
your name in stars
to dance that autumn well.

Terence Brick,
Arts Workshop,
Newbury

At school a master gave me a piece of advice. He told me
to read the question on an exam paper and then figure how
I could turn it so that I could write the answers I knew.

In other words, take a title and figure how it can fit with
what you want to write.

Titles are at best indicators. Sometimes they tell the reader
more or less what's to follow, at other times they're down-
right confusing.

As it happens I like titles. Go. Choose a title that amuses
you then let the words fly.

I Is Not Necessarily Me

Style is synthetic; and the artist, seeking, so to speak, a peg to plait about, takes up at once two or more elements or two or more views of the subject in hand; combines, implicates, and contrasts them; and while, in one sense, he was merely seeking an occasion for the necessary knot, he will be found, in the other, to have greatly enriched the meaning ...

Robert Louis Stevenson

Never be afraid of using 'I' in writing. Unless you are being especially confessional the reader usually takes on the role cast by the first person singular. As I mentioned in an earlier chapter, the would-be writer worries that their work will be too personal when in fact once the work is on the page and then maybe printed the 'I' has passed into the common domain.

'I' does not necessarily mean the writing is confessional. Probably it is used most often as the narrator. Here's the opening of one of my favourite books, 'Moby Dick' by Herman Melville. This is how he introduces the reader to the narrator. 'Call me Ishmael. Some years ago – never mind how long precisely – having little or no money in my purse, and nothing particular to interest me on shore, I thought I would sail about a little and see the watery part of the world.'

Although the use of 'I' can be fine and effective nonetheless a piece of writing may be made more dramatic, have a totally different slant, if it is cast in a different mood by using 'he', 'she', 'we' or 'they'. In some writing there is no need for the personal pronoun at all.

Poets often use 'I' when they write about an object.

In the following examples 'I' is a bridge, a stone, a wall:

Bridge at Lumb

I am the bridge
At Lumb, by Dill Scout's Wood, Jack Bridge,
Top o'th'Hill and Hoar Side Moor.

Black as carbon, Colden Water
Laps against the pitted piers,
Rides the river.

Down the mill race foaming water
Moves the man-made patterns; listen –
Hear the music.

Chimneys, black smoke, stone on metal,
Weary clog-step waking dreaming –
Not in this place.

Sunshine greens through birch and willow,
Grasses, ferns, cow parsley, nettles,
Leaflight blinds me.

I am the bridge
At Lumb, by wood and water crowned;
You touch the stone, the wheel stops turning.

> Judith Pollard,
> Arvon Course at Lumb Bank

The Chronicles of a Stone

A druid's diamond,
A sacrificial stone,
I was used at first as
A heathen monument.
Around me, scratching chalk screams
And mountains cry.

Then a Tudor witness
As smooth as glass, hearthstone,
I listen during banquets

Submerged in a hell-like furnace;
An endless torment
Till the mortals leave.

Promoted to mantel
In a Royalist Hall,
A stone image
Of a saint repelling evil:
Ironic, since I
Once flowed with blood.

I observed the Roundheads,
Occupy the stronghold
In the name of their God,
Impale the cavalier in hate
Execute the staff
In Lord Cromwell's name.

The decades inched by,
Evolving into decades,
While the humans progress
Building weapons for destruction
To stop the stone of civilisation
And make me sand.

Gary Maclachlan,
Bishop Wordsworth's School,
Salisbury

The Wall

I stand motionless, with no characteristic of cloud.
Only the rustle of ivy stirs me
in the bitter wind.
I gaze fixedly at boot and sandal
eroding the gravel base on which I was built.
One day, by shrub or shovel
the scene may change.

I watch and observe the children
aim a football towards me.
Pain does not strike me, instead

envy flares inside me,
not being able to
join the frantic play.

I call out.
My voice is captured in the wind,
disappearing into the large space around me,
the wide, empty world which I cannot see,
which I will never see.
Wanderlust strikes me deeply.

I hear the voices of people
call to each other,
never blinking an eyelid at the
dirty slab in front of them.
I let the unheard groan fall
from hunched brick, chapped lips,
to let people know my spirits
are lowered.
To tell them I am transfixed.

Greg Swetman,
Arvon Course at Totleigh Barton;
Castle School,
Taunton

Take a piece of your writing, verse or prose, and try casting it another way. If you've used 'I' see what happens when you change to 'he' or 'she', 'we' or 'they'. Is it more dramatic or less? Some writing requires no pronouns. The thing to do is experiment.

Nourish the Senses

... if you meditate a work of art, you should first long roll the subject under the tongue to make sure you like the flavour, before you brew a volume that shall taste of it from end to end; or if you propose to enter on the field of controversy, you should first have thought upon the question under all conditions, in health as well as in sickness, in sorrow as well as in joy.

Robert Louis Stevenson

See. Hear. Smell. Touch. Taste. These are the five senses. Why are they so valuable to the writer? Because by use of the senses a writer is able to give a living vitality to what is being written about. You see an object so precisely that all the textures of it are printed on your mind. When you hear, the listening absorbs everything – loud or quiet, near or far. The smell evokes pleasure or dislike and more besides. Touch tells us how hard, soft, hot, cold, rough, smooth and so on. Then there's taste. I guess you can work out how many differences taste tells us.

Write out five sentences, one for each of the senses. In the first, describe accurately an object you see – really see. Then do the same with the other four senses.

You could, for instance, take a feather and subject it to a thorough going-over through your senses. Or try a piece of bread.

Don't write neat sentences immediately. Activate the senses first. Make jottings. List the object's attributes, then, when you've captured the whole thing, you can start to describe it.

When you feel confident that your senses are working for you, you might try writing a description of:

The Inside of a Car
A Railway Platform
Patch of Hedgerow
Aisle in a Supermarket.

As an echo to the five senses, remember to use the Who, What, When, Why and Where's. In some sorts of writing, stories particularly, these questions can help the student construct a blueprint for a piece of work.

Some examples of the use of senses:

Haiku

I touch wood, climb fir
Feel salt wind freshen my hair
Smell the rough white sea.

> Mukti Mitchell,
> The Small School,
> Hartland

I hear skeletons rattling
like a baby's rattle
at the graveyard.

> Balakrishna McAlinn,
> Rhyme Roundabout,
> Newbury Arts Workshop

Country Cottage

Wooden beams dark with smoke
sag, tortured by feet.
Their pegged benevolence harbours
past lives, old deaths.
The scent of hanging hams
mingled with herbs
gives way to filtered coffee
and Dutch cigars.

Lintels twist, scorched
by centuries of fires
that spat with game;
hooks hanging with pots
of simple sustenance.
Now they are hung with horsebrass,
the confines filled with terracotta urns,
controlled smoke.

Liz McCrum,
Arvon Course at Totleigh Barton;
Castle School,
Taunton

The Meal (Extract)

... It was a beautiful June evening. The hawthorn mingled its fragrance with the lilac bush outside the door. A slight breeze whispered through the pear blossom, breathing confetti-like flakes on to the lawn. In the distance a robin chirruped a disembodied song. It was as if they had ordered this evening; night was falling with its smells of newly laundered clothes. If this was entertaining the boss, Sue thought, there was nothing to it.

Suddenly, from over the wall came a shuffling, dragging sound, then a thump. However, the beef was spitting in its dish, around which were plump potatoes freckled with juice, and a large Yorkshire pudding like a brown rippled lake was waiting to be served. An artist mixing her palette, Sue passed around the dishes, admiring her contrasting colours of sprouts and carrots. They were sitting around a pine table, with best pottery and spring flowers. Red wine gleamed in clear crystal; international and business relationships were fused. She smiled – the beef was not full of gristle and the Yorkshire pudding had not sunk.

After serving the apple pie and clotted Devon cream, she became aware of a slight scraping under the table. She looked at the heavy hanging cloth, and to her horror saw her innocent-eyed, pure white Persian cat eating her neighbour's pet duck. She threw down the table cloth; her ears buzzed, her heart thumped, as, with a less than healthy sensation in her stomach, she tried to be calm. Above the table was normality and ordered hospitality; beneath was a picture of disorganised hell. The windpipe, ripped open by needle-sharp fangs, revealed veins and sinews which mocked the civilisation of candles and wine, while the polite, mannered ceremony between hosts and guests seemed on an entirely different plane to the concentrated, single-minded efforts of beast devouring fowl.

'What lovely pastry,' Reza was saying, while all the time Sue could hear the rustling beneath, shutting out for her the polished courtesy of table small-talk.

She rose to put on a tape. 'The apples come from our garden,' she said, hoping to drown the noise by her banalities, but inside her head was the interminable scratching and tearing. Even Bob Dylan's raucous voice seemed at that moment totally civilised in contrast to the sight she had seen.

Nobody noticed, or if they did, were too polite to comment. Paul, who might have said something, was at the opposite end of the table.

'How many times can a man turn his head,' Dylan was whining, 'and pretend that he just doesn't see?' Sue decided something had to be done. 'Paul, would you help me with the coffee?' They went into the kitchen together ...

Jan Cooper,
'Teachers as Writers' Course,
Menai Centre,
Anglesey

For the reader/writer who has come along this far I hope that the notebook abounds with words and bulges with drafts, that the well chosen word, phrase, sentence, has turned into a pleasing stanza, paragraph, and finally into finished poem or story. I wouldn't want to say that writing gets easier but I can suggest that once the writer has discovered the jigsawing of the best words into their best order, he or she will read the work with more approval.

It is gratifying to know that something you've written

and fine-tuned gives a reader or listener somewhere pleasure or whatever you intended they should feel. But it's as well to know that there are critics who would make Mac the Knife seem like a mild-mannered vicar. Nobody said it was going to be easy.

Go To It

Literature, like any other art, is singularly interesting to the artist; and, in a degree peculiar to itself among the arts, it is useful to mankind. These are the sufficient justifications for any young man or woman who adopts it as the business of his life. I shall not say much about the wages. A writer can live by his writing. If not so luxuriously as by other trades, then less luxuriously. The nature of the work he does all day will more affect his happiness than the quality of his dinner at night.

Robert Louis Stevenson

Time: it does take time to write words, phrases, sentences, paragraphs, chapters – a whole story or verse or play, or whatever. Getting used to taking time out of the day so that one can write can be tricky. To begin with it might seem self-indulgent, even selfish, but once that time, say twenty minutes out of the twenty-four hours, is put aside and kept aside, the busy household will get used to the idea. It is quite salutary to find that the rest of the world revolves intact without one during that time.

Place: a place to write is a luxury. To find enough room to have a table and chair where one can leave notebook and paper knowing they will not be disturbed is a kind of heaven for the writer. Otherwise a drawing board to rest on the arms of a chair is comfortable. Anywhere one can find space to rest a notebook and be undisturbed for a spate of time is good news. The place to write is the place to write. Like the right words, the right place needs to be found.

Notebook: it's easier to keep writings together in a note-book. Bits of paper have a tendency to fly around and lose themselves.

Pen: some people have a fetish about pens. If pens are

95

important then make sure you have one you like, if not just be sure it works.

Dictionary: O.E.D., Collins, Chambers, Webster's.

Roget's Thesaurus of English Words and Phrases.

Brewer's Dictionary of Phrase and Fable.

Fowler's Modern English Usage.

Typewriter: if you would like your work to be read, it will sometime need to be typed. In any case it is easier to work on the draft of a piece of writing when it is typed. It is easier to read but also it is removed from the impact and self identity of handwriting. Nowadays a number of people use word processors – that's fine if you've got one and know how to use it.

Sending writing out: don't be too hasty. When you're ready, and prepared for the inevitable rejection slip, type the work out with double spacing and good margins. You shouldn't be too miserly with paper. Target the publisher, magazine, paper, by doing some research. This means finding out which ones publish the type of work compatible with your own. So visit the library and check through likely publications. There's the Writers' and Artists' Yearbook which lists names and addresses of publishers, magazines and papers. And the Poetry Society (21 Earls Court Square, London SW5 9DE) has its own list.

Should you wish to send out a novel or collection of writings it is courteous and wise to send a letter to the publisher asking whether they would like to read the work. Enclose a brief synopsis with the letter. Always enclose a stamped addressed envelope.

When sending out a manuscript be sure to keep a carbon or photocopy (floppy disc?).

With poems it's usual to send between three and six to a magazine. Again enclose a SAE.

There are books which deal with particular aspects of writing in the series called The Way to Write:

The Way to Write
The Way to Write Poetry

96

The Way to Write Novels
The Way to Write for Television
The Way to Write for Children
The Way to Write Short Stories.

These are also published by Elm Tree.

From here on it's practice and more practice.

Usually in all works of art that have been conceived from within outwards, and generously nourished from the author's mind, the moment in which he begins to execute is one of extreme perplexity and strain. Artists of indifferent energy and an imperfect devotion to their own ideal make this ungrateful effort once for all; and, having formed a style, adhere to it through life. But those of a higher order cannot rest content with a process which, as they continue to employ it, must infallibly degenerate towards the academic and the cut-and-dried. Every fresh work in which they embark is the signal for a fresh engagement of the whole forces of their mind; and the changing views which accompany the growth of their experience are marked by still more sweeping alterations in the manner of their art.

Robert Louis Stevenson.